GARDENS IN EMBROIDERY

Hidcote Garden. The fabric ground is dyed and embroidered by hand. The lettering is worked over a 'waste' canvas, which is then pulled away, giving accurate lettering on a fabric ground. Worked from the illustration on page 40 (Marilyn Phipps)

GARDENS IN EMBROIDERY

Val Holmes

B. T. Batsford Ltd, London

ISBN 0 7134 5994 8

Typeset by Latimer Trend & Company Ltd
Printed in Hong Kong
for the publishers
B. T. Batsford Ltd
4 Fitzhardinge Street
London W1H 0AH

RIGHT:
Collection of knot garden and parterre designs
from contemporary source books
and gardens still in existence

CONTENTS

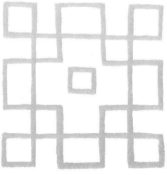

ACKNOWLEDGEMENTS

I would like to thank all the friends and students who contributed work to the book, much of which was done specially. I have aimed to acknowledge all work shown, but have failed to do so with colour plates on page 19 which were completed in a design school. I apologise to the person who worked these paintings, as I have not been able to trace her name – my memory of her leads me to believe she will forgive me! I am grateful to Martin (my husband and 'the engineer') for all his help and encouragement, and to friends who read the book and helped with layout. Credits for photography and printing are as follows: garden photography by the author, printed by Bob Garnett; all black and white embroidery photography and printing was by Bob Garnett except the reproductions of Sonya Head's embroidery, which were by Ron Head; the colour photography was done by many of the contributors, myself and, of course, Bob Garnett, whose work and encouragement were essential to the book.

AUTHOR'S NOTE

What I have attempted to write is the content of a design school I have been running for a number of years which takes gardens as a starting point for embroidery design. Detailed embroidery techniques are not included as it is assumed that embroiderers will already have some skills and knowledge, and that the further reading list at the end of the book will provide information on any unfamiliar techniques.

INTRODUCTION

A very short history

BEAUTIFUL gardens, well-kept and ordered or appealingly disordered, have fascinated people for centuries. A tidy garden shows human beings as controllers of the nature that perhaps attempts to engulf from the other side of the fence; yet when a garden looks attractive all year round we admire the knowledge of nature's whims that can create such an effect. Perhaps gardens epitomise both our struggle with and desire to conquer nature, and our ability and need to work with it.

Garden design has tended to follow the modes of thinking and way of life of contemporary society. It is affected not simply by advances in techniques of cultivation and the availability of plant species, but more especially by trends in architecture which influence the surrounding landscape. Fashions in thinking have an important bearing on how ordered or rural a garden is expected to look, and on how it relates as a living space.

There is evidence of gardens and courtyards with ponds, fish, fruit trees and plants dating from thousands of years BC. Illustrations in frescoes and paintings from early Egyptian times to later Islamic cultures survive in museum records.

Research on how gardens were constructed, and on what they may have contained, has been advanced by

the ruins of Roman villas, which probably once had a formal area with hedge-lined paths and lawns with ornamental fountains, as well as informal terraces planted with trees and shrubs.

During the Renaissance, garden design took on a new importance. The knot garden style developed from the courtyards of monastery kitchen gardens. Laid beds in intricate patterns characterised many gardens in Elizabethan England and across Northern Europe. The late seventeenth century saw a fashion for extended vistas, parterres (ornamental arrangements of hedges and flower beds), fountains and cascades.

The Baroque brought a new grandeur to garden design as the formal garden extended to include geometric groves and avenues.

In the eighteenth century there was an English reaction against such taming of nature and formalisation, and the landscape garden emerged in the form of rolling grassland, often dotted with appropriate animals, giving way here and there to small groups of trees and irregular stretches of water, with bridges and small buildings added to create a classical landscape merging with the surrounding countryside in the manner of the popular painters of the day.

The turn of the nineteenth century saw a further reaction, this time turning against such rusticity

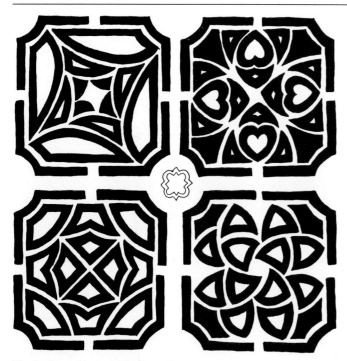

The Gardens of Love at Villandry in France.
TOP LEFT: **L'Amour Tragique.** The box is pruned into the shape of blades, swords and daggers. It is filled with red flowers and represents the blood spilled because of women
BOTTOM LEFT: **L'Amour Adultère.** Horns and fans (recalling the flirtatiousness of their use), and in the centre 'billets doux' which an inconsistent woman would despatch, pledging loyalty. The predominant colour is yellow – the symbol of betrayed love
TOP RIGHT: **L'Amour Tendre.** Hearts are separated by orange flames of love. In the centre masques are represented which allow whispers of tenderness unseen
BOTTOM RIGHT: **L'Amour Passionné** is represented by hearts shattered by passion. Their placing evokes a sense of dance, and it is at balls and masques that so many promises are made and broken. The colours in this garden are mixed, as passions are uneven

towards the idea of a more ornamental garden extending away from the house.

The Victorians chose to mix a variety of styles in their interiors and this was also true of their garden design, which included every type of bed, cast-iron ornaments, rockwork, shrubberies, ferneries and ground carpet bedding of the nature now reserved for municipal parks.

As the century progressed an argument developed between the craftsmen and the trained artist/designers, who probably knew little about the tools of the trade. This also occurred in gardening, where similar comparisons were drawn between the architect, who could plan the formal layout a garden needed, and the gardener with his intimate knowledge of garden materials. A resolution was sought in a formal layout of hedges and walls around a cottage style of informal borders, so that nature was allowed to soften man-made designs.

This is perhaps the concept of gardening that we hold today, but to it we have added the continental and oriental notion that a garden can be used as a living area and an extension of the home. Our formal areas for living and playing take the form of patios or areas of lawn; either may be broken up with areas of formal or informal planting which may be large or small – the choice is often dependent upon the amount of time that is available to look after the garden. We have discovered that by a combination of careful design and knowledge of plants it is possible to have a formal or more informal, or even wild, garden in whatever space is available.

*   *   *

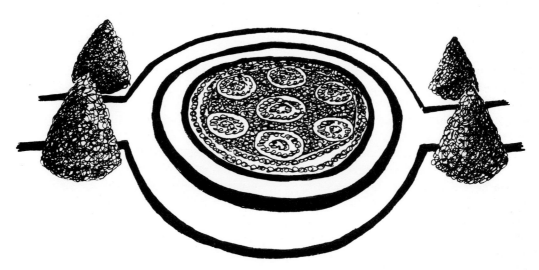

The restored seventeenth-century parterre at the Chateau of Angers, France. The restoration shows an interest in nineteenth-century carpet bedding, which is as popular with French municipalities as it is in England

Plants and gardens have been subjects for embroiderers for as long as history relates. The symbolism and patterns of fruits and flowers have always been important in all branches of the arts, and was particularly so to Tudor and Stuart embroiderers. The opulence and splendour of full-blown blooms were an inspiration to eighteenth-century stitchers and, later, the Victorians. From formal patterns which concentrate on the plant forms or arrangement of the garden, to an interest in the naturalism of landscape gardens, or the colours and charm of a cottage garden, embroidery and gardening have followed fashion hand in hand.

Today gardens, like interiors, are arranged in a wide variety of styles, and embroidery can adopt the same attitude. The most essential criterion for embroidery today is that it be creative and original. To this end, gardens can offer a valuable starting point in the search for inspiration. The different problems which arise for the artist and embroiderer, associated with the use of tone, form, texture, colour, choice of subject matter and composition, can all be met and tackled within the context of the garden. A beginner may find that a careful choice of subject matter, perhaps concentrating on a small area at first, will bring rewards. The more experienced embroiderer will also find challenges which may relate to scale, depth of field, colour experimentation or techniques used.

Gardens offer an excellent starting point for experimenting with new media and the novice has an excellent chance of coming to grips with mark-making or drawing, design and innovation in a textile medium, as the subject of gardens can be easily broken down into areas of study that can be approached individually, so that skills can be mastered gradually and eventually more ambitious projects explored.

*   *   *

Many embroiderers find gardening to be a natural extension of their talents and interests, and I have friends who have designed their own gardens in order to offer a source of inspiration for their embroidery. If the time or space is not available to create such a garden for yourself, there are many gardens open to the public.

The National Gardens Scheme, which is a charitable trust, publishes a list of gardens and their open days throughout England and Wales. It refers not only to larger and more professionally kept gardens, but also to open days when the gardens of a whole village may be open for charity – a scheme which provides an opportunity to see and record ideas which may be a little out of the ordinary. The National Trust Handbook also contains a wealth of information for garden

An herbaceous border in a cottage garden set alongside a stone path

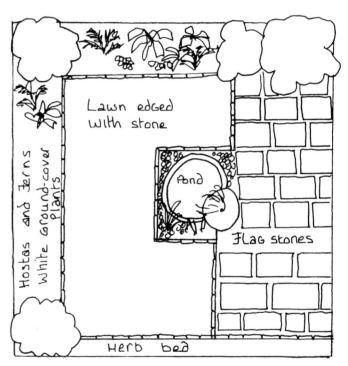

This plan of a contemporary garden provides seating space in an area of calm whites and greens, with the relaxing sensation of running water. These qualities, set within an ordered framework, could be a suitable starting point for a restful embroidery

visitors. It may be worth becoming a member if you have a good National Trust garden nearby, so that further visits can be made and observations and drawing need not be hurried. I am lucky enough to live near Hidcote Gardens, which are certainly worth repeated visits. There are many other publications available on open gardens. Some of the commercial lists include photographs and good descriptions of the gardens, which are useful if you are looking for something specific.

When visiting a garden, especially if your intention is to draw or paint, try to choose a day and time when the garden will be at its quietest – mornings in midweek are by far the best! Even for photography, it is much easier to work when the garden is empty, as photographs will not have to be rushed in an effort to ensure 'garden only' shots. If you are intimidated by

LEFT: This oil pastel was worked from the watercolour sketch of Le Parc des Moutiers on page 65. I attempted to capture the heat of the day and the colours and qualities of this marvellous house and gardens throughout the year as well as the impression gained of Monet's work and garden and the work of the Impressionists, some of whom lived and worked around Dieppe

RIGHT: This small machine embroidery worked on coloured scrim without any backing fabric represents the small works that preceded **Le Parc des Moutiers – an Impression** embroidery (by the author)

The pond area at Ilmington Manor, where the hard edges of the pond, wall and paving are softened through the use of plants

11

the thought of people looking over your shoulder, choose a quiet spot away from the main traffic. If all else fails, stare steadfastly at your drawing and ignore all remarks – people will normally only speak to you if they can make eye contact so you should be able to achieve an uninterrupted session by this method. The most important thing is not to give up; very few people are 'born' artists or embroiderers!

Practice and determination are essential if good results are to be obtained, but the careful choice of materials is also important. Learning what can be achieved with different media by practising before

working directly from life can also boost confidence. Practise mark-making, colour mixing and learning to handle a brush or pencil.

When deciding to draw outside, set aside a special day and stick to it. It is very easy to find excuses for avoiding things that appear difficult and new. Having tried drawing 'in the field' once, your confidence will increase and drawing will even seem quite enjoyable. The marks and images made in the garden will gradually become relevant, necessary and innovative for your embroidery, and these first horror-struck tentative steps will fade into a distant memory.

This was a first attempt, drawn by an engineer used to pens but unused to drawing from subjects! But careful observation has given a charm to this drawing, and the pot has almost a cartoon-like quality

1

STARTING OUT

Materials for mark-making and recording visual information

MANY people first become interested in embroidery through the successful completion of a kit, and would like to work something more personal or unique, or perhaps would like to experiment a little with the techniques they have learned. Embroiderers who have always designed their own work may find that an approach which includes drawing and design work before a needle is even lifted can improve the originality and the overall effect of their final pieces of work.

This chapter introduces the basic art materials and shows how they can be used to record visual information which can in turn be used as a starting point for embroidery design. I refer to this process as 'mark-making' as it is important to bear in mind that your drawings do not have to win any art competitions. Paperwork has, however, to give good quality information for the final embroidery, the design and technique of which will emerge from the nature of the marks made.

Mark-making does not have to be approached with the notion of creating a finished product, but simply a collection of marks, textures, lines, shapes and possibly colours, although composition may become important.

Mark-making can certainly be fun, and is very inspirational for original embroideries, but a loose and unselfconscious approach to drawing seems impossible for many, especially those used to a neat and orthodox approach to embroidery. The usual cry is 'I can't draw', but this is not in fact the case. The phrase ought to be, 'I can't look'. As the subject is more and more carefully observed, the juxtaposition of shapes and colours, the relationship of one tone against another or the subtlety of available lines or textures is gradually noticed with increasing confidence. As a result, the subject matter is understood more thoroughly than would be possible by any other means, such as photography or using other illustrations. It is this thorough-looking and real understanding that lies behind adequate drawing. By learning to observe well, it is possible to begin to master the materials and produce good useful drawings and paintings for use in embroidery.

Many people use just a camera for recording information. Although it can be a useful tool, the camera should not be relied upon too heavily, as it can offer only a limited way of seeing a subject, and the interpretation that will be offered will have fewer possibilities than the more personally influenced paperwork you should learn to achieve. However, photography can be useful for recording images when time is limited, or if colour is required and only

monochromatic drawings can be made. It can also be used for recording difficult aspects of foreground flowers.

Photography is also an excellent way of mastering composition. Looking through a viewfinder and carefully composing each shot improves appreciation of the problems associated with good composition: contrast in scale, shapes, textures, colour and depth of field, the position of focal points and so on.

Photography can be a minefield with the wide choice and technical data available today, so here is a brief guide. An additional reading list is suggested for further information.

Photography

Photography can be an expensive 'hobby' if the information recorded is to be of a high enough calibre. A good camera is essential, as it is important to have as much control over the picture as possible. Although simple cameras may be good for taking family snaps, a single lens reflex camera (usually abbreviated to SLR) is virtually a must for recording good quality visual information, although top of the range 35 mm compact cameras now offer a good standard of image.

The main benefit of a SLR camera is that the view through the viewfinder is through the lens of the camera, thus avoiding mistakes such as cutting out items that are meant to be included: what is seen will be the resulting picture. Buying good quality film and having large, clear prints processed can also be expensive, but must be budgeted for – it is important to be able to take a lot of pictures without being intimidated by the thought that every shot must be successful and useful.

It is preferable to have a manually focused camera, as it is then possible not only to pick out precisely which part of the image is to be the sharpest, but also to see how the rest of the image is likely to appear. It is often useful to take one photograph with the foreground in focus, and another of the same view but focusing on the background. This approach may also offer ideas for embroideries.

If the range in focus is to be increased (the depth of field of a picture), this can be achieved by using a smaller aperture (the amount by which the lens is open, known as 'F stop') and a faster film (films are

ABOVE LEFT: A border with the foreground in focus

LEFT: The same view with the foreground out of focus, as the distance is sharpened into focus

marked with an ASA which indicates their speed – 100 is most usual, but a higher number will increase the aperture rating and thus improve the depth of field). If a sharply focused foreground against a blurred background is required, a lower F stop is desirable.

A trellis on a sloping roof with frosted clematis leaves climbing over it

BELOW: This close-up could inspire a three-dimensional embroidery on a groundwork of trellising. Lace worked on the sewing machine might capture the mood and cobweb qualities of a frosty morning

Choose a camera with control of aperture settings if at all possible. The appropriate shutter speed (the amount of time the shutter is open and the film exposed to light) can be chosen on most modern cameras. It is important to check which shutter speed is being used, as if it is too slow the image can be blurred. I find I cannot hold a camera still and be sure of a clear image below one-thirtieth of a second, and a faster speed than this is usually desirable, especially if anything that may move is included.

Most importantly, take notes of all the steps taken for each photograph: the film used, the aperture and shutter speed employed, where the film was developed, the weather and so on. Eventually the formula that works best for the images desired will become apparent from the notes.

The major problem with a photographic image is that, although its choice is personal, it may lack the essential detail and information required for the type of embroidery desired. Its exact realism can also be a problem for many people, who automatically produce a piece of work that is merely a reproduction of the original image. This may be all right, but it is exciting to experiment with the perception of reality and the use of techniques which can blur or define certain elements. Although interesting and innovative work

The foreground of leaves in front of the camera are out of focus — the shapes have merely blank tonal qualities and lack texture. Against the highly textured background this feature acts as a relief. A busy embroidery could be worked with blank spaces left where the leaf shapes occur to give a negative impact on the background, or the shapes could be added to an embroidered ground in relief. The potager at Barnsley House, Gloucestershire

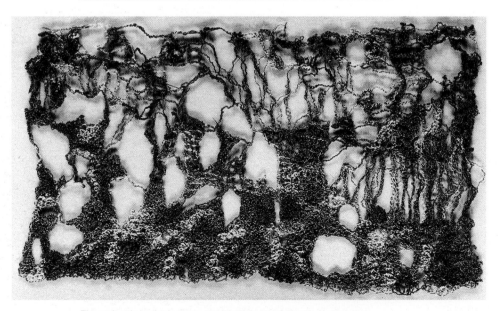

This embroidery sample shows the development of this idea, where the foreground blur of shape has been left as spaces in the lace structure. Worked by machine on hot-water vanishing fabric (by the author)

can be produced from photographs (the work in chapter 7 was largely based on a photographic image) the most satisfactory way of producing work that is essentially your own is to be in complete control of the images produced from the start. This, of course, means drawing yourself!

'Drawing' and 'design' are two words that many people have been scared of since their schooldays, but this is unnecessary. First, remember that the completed drawing will not be entered for any fine art competition. You may be the only person to see it: it is, after all, the final piece of embroidery that will be displayed, and the drawing is only a means to an end. Secondly, any worry arising from lack of familiarity with the art media can be cured by careful exercises.

The following sections give a brief introduction to mark-making materials. Mark-making that you have already practised in the process of embroidery can aid the mark-making on paper and provide useful experience and information. But to become aware of the possibilities of each medium so that it can be better used it is necessary to learn its capabilities through experimentation and the understanding of its nature. Let us start with the most basic medium of all – the pencil.

Using pencils

Pencils are graded from very hard (6H) through to very soft (6B, although 9B is also available). The soft range of pencils is best for drawing purposes, so start with a selection from B to 6B. A selection of papers with different qualities of roughness in whites to off-whites will also be useful.

Now start experimenting. Try using the same pressure with each pencil on different papers to see what types of mark they can achieve. Then vary the pressure with each pencil; try altering it midway through a line or scribble, as well as drawing whole lines or filling whole areas with one pressure. A greater variety of tone can be achieved with softer pencils, but firmer, finer lines are possible with harder ones. Always have a pencil sharpener to hand as it is essential to keep a good point on pencils to achieve the best and most controlled results, although a very soft blunt pencil can be useful for laying down large areas of shading.

Having experimented thus far, try ways of controlling shading. A line can change from soft to dark and can thus give an indication of a light source. To achieve a controlled all-over effect with shading, it is often best not to confine the direction of the marks. Orderly scribbles in different directions can give a smooth transition between tonal values as the shading is gradually built up in lightly applied layers. Again, try

different grades of pencil to discover the difference in results. Also try using lines, scribbles and crosshatching as means of indicating shade.

Smooth shade created with a pencil will be reminiscent of the qualities that are achieved by layering see-through fabrics, dyeing (try spraying and using masks and stencils), or close stitching by hand or machine. Experiments with lines and scribbles will probably bring to mind bolder creations of marks and stitches.

Creating tonal drawings with different media

Following the guidelines and experiments for pencils, try some of the following: charcoal, conté, various thicknesses of fibre-tip pen, and pen and wash.

Each of these has its own characteristics which will be discovered through experimentation, but the following guidelines may also help.

Charcoal

Choose a variety of thicknesses for ease of use, and small lengths of 5–8 cm (2–3 in). Charcoal can be messy and difficult to use, but by using large sheets of paper and working at arm's length this problem can be overcome. Charcoal can be easily smudged, which is both an advantage and a disadvantage. If a smudge is to indicate an area of shade, try to keep it as controlled as possible and include linear work in the drawing to maintain clarity (at least initially). Charcoal can be removed to a certain extent with a putty rubber (available from most art shops) which is also useful for reducing unwanted amounts of shading in pencil. Smudges and fingerprints can also be cleaned up when the work is finished. Fixative spray can be added at any stage, to preserve a satisfactory area and prevent further smudging, or after the work is finished. Charcoal can be a useful medium to work in if your natural inclination towards drawing is inhibited.

Conté

Named after its inventor, conté is a mixture of graphite, clay, water and paste produced in square sticks. Originally made in sepia, white, grey and black, a variety of colours are now available and can be used like pastels. For drawing purposes it works in monochrome like a cross between charcoal and pencil. Conté and charcoal are best used to create the mood of a garden rather than to explain the whereabouts of detail.

Pens

There are many makes of fine nib, continuous-flow pens on the market which are very suitable for working in fine detail, or for making marks directly

B pencil   2B pencil   4B pencil   6B pencil

Experiments with pencils using different pressure, marks and shading techniques. Shading becomes smoother with a softer pencil, lines can be more controlled with a harder one. Such work will increase confidence in the use of pencils for drawing actual subject matter

These two paintings are worked from the same image using different gauges of paintbrush to obtain a more orderly or freer effect

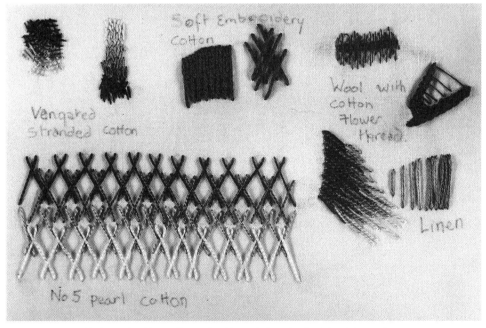

Marks made with pencils translated into stitch marks. Straight stitches and herringbone are used in cottons, wools and linens on a cotton ground (by the author)

associated with the textures present in a garden. Coarser pens are also useful for rough, lively images, and various grades of pen can be mixed well to create feelings of depth or scale. Experiment with marks and textures and try these out in hand or machine stitchery.

Pens have the advantage of being permanent, and, although this sounds terrifying to the novice, it is very useful to practise with a medium that cannot be erased as this can increase confidence and produce more self-assured drawings.

Many fibre-tip pens will run if water is applied to them with a brush, and this can be a more convenient format than pen and ink wash if you are drawing in the garden.

Experiment with the different thicknesses of pen available, the kinds of marks and lines they can make by using different pressures, and the sort of qualities that can be added by using different papers – from rough water-colour to smooth shiny surfaces.

This drawing using calligraphic fibre-tip pens on a rough watercolour paper gives a finish reminiscent of charcoal. The marks are made quickly and decisively, although each mark is thought out carefully before being drawn (by the author)

ABOVE: This charcoal drawing shows the atmospheric qualities that can be achieved in this medium

RIGHT: Shape, line and some texture are important to this pen and wash drawing. Distance is indicated by less clear shapes in the background. The wash is used to indicate shade and shadow cast by the light source which is obviously above the subject (by the author)

Pencil crayons

Pencil crayons are probably the most widely available medium for adding colour to drawings, but it is important to buy a set of artist's quality crayons. There are crayons available that will run in water, but this is less essential than producing a good quality finish when used dry, although the variety of possible marks is increased, and these crayons can also prove useful for adding more life to worksheets. Check that softly shaded qualities can be produced with the crayons, as well as heavier, stronger marks. Choose a box of

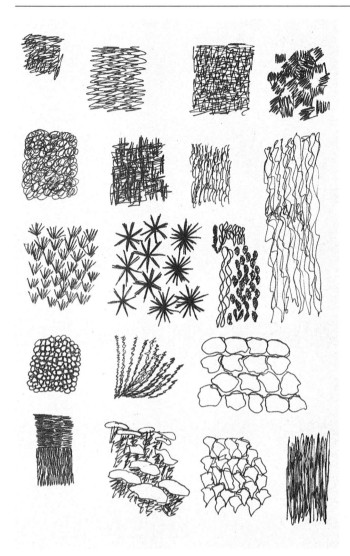

Samples of marks and textures that might be suitable for garden drawings made with a pen

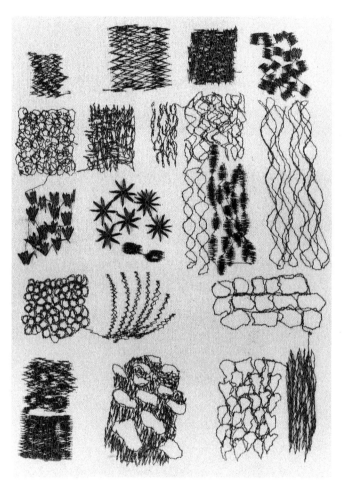

Sample in free machine embroidery from the pen-mark sample. Starting top left: **1** Zigzag up and down with rows of diagonal zigzag **2** Open zigzag up and down **3** Zigzag up and down and then across horizontally **4** Closed zigzag blocks in different directions **5** Circling around with straight stitch **6** Moving vertically then horizontally intermittently (weave stitch) **7** Drawing small loops with a straight stitch **8** and **9** Using a 'wave' stitch setting **10** Steps of zigzag with the needle in the fabric as it is moved round **11** Creating flowers with the needle in the centre each time the fabric is moved, the fabric is kept still for each petal – the two samples at the base of this section are of a circular motion drawn with a zigzag setting **12** Using a 'leaf' stitch setting, although this can be done by changing the width setting **13** Drawing circles with a straight stitch **14** Fine zigzag drawing lines and then retracing steps **15** Drawing 'bricks' with a straight stitch **16** Closed zigzag in lines **17** Shapes drawn, larger in foreground, straight lines in between **18** Leaf shapes drawn with a straight stitch **19** Straight stitch up and down unevenly

Materials for colour drawing and painting

Adopting an experimental approach will help in getting acquainted with the many media that can be used for colour drawing and painting.

Colour has a way of speaking for itself, and gardens are an excellent subject for learning about colour and colour mixing, so when faced with a border brimming with colour, really looking and obtaining the nuances in colour and mark will give surprisingly good and useful results in the drawing.

First, let us consider the most usual colour media.

ABOVE: Oil painting, **Wisteria**. The methods for this and the embroidery are discussed in the section on hanging gardens in Chapter 8 (Richard Box)

RIGHT: Collage and embroidery of **Wisteria**. Different coloured fabrics are glued to a hessian base which is then treated with hand and machine stitchery (Richard Box)

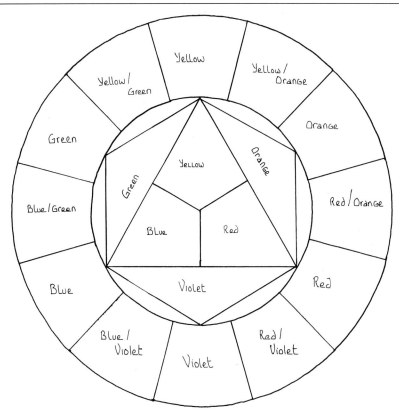

A colour circle with notes on colour position. The inner circle contains the primary colours. The hexagon continues with the secondary colours. The colours opposite in the circle are complementary. Any pair of complementaries will always contain the three primary colours, e.g. Red/Green (Blue+Yellow). The warm part of the colour circle is around red/orange, the cool part around blue/green. Yellow appears to be the brightest colour, violet the dullest – hence their very effective use to describe light and shade

colours carefully; you may later regret not having bought enough colours. It is possible to buy boxes with seventy-two or more colours, although this is probably excessive. Choose a box with thirty-six or forty-eight coloured pencils. The smaller the range, the more frustrating obtaining observed colours can be, although mixing from a limited range will provide a lot of insight when it comes to mixing threads together for a colour effect. Soft crayons mix well when layered on paper, and water-soluble ones can also be layered and mixed with a wet brush. Using colour added in layers, rather than just using the colour 'straight', will improve the interest in a drawing.

Drawing in pencil and then 'colouring in' with crayon is not the ideal way of producing a piece of work: the result can often be stilted, tight and uninteresting. Practise working in crayons alone, producing the lines as needed or, preferably, using no lines at all. It is possible to shade up to edges by using a piece of paper as a mask or stencil to create a firm edge without a line. A softer edge can be achieved by tearing the paper to be used as the mask.

Experiment on a variety of collected papers and try pressing on them in a hard and soft manner, producing strong marks and areas of colour as well as soft pastel shading. We are taught from an early age to use pencils gently, but they can provide exciting and more intensely colourful results when applied with harder marks, or built up in layers of colour.

Overlaying colour, which is a method largely associated with painting techniques, works well with pencil crayons. Start by laying down an area of colour, say yellow, then try adding other colours on top in soft strokes. Red will give an orangey tone, blue will give green. The complementary shade (the opposite on a colour circle) will create a 'shadow' much more effectively than the addition of black, more of the same colour, or brown, which is often chosen! Cooler colours will also create a notion of shadow or depth (these are the colours around the blue/green area of the colour circle), and warm colours (those around red/orange, especially yellow) will give a greater sense of sunlight and closeness. Try adding these in layers to other colours already laid down.

Fibre-tip pens

Fibre-tip pens tend to have an on/off quality: they either make a fairly strong mark or none at all. As with pen and ink, working in coloured pens can increase confidence, and as long as the work is not thrown away as soon as something seems to go wrong, but an effort is made to continue to create a valid piece of work, a great deal can be learned about colour and mark.

As with pencils, experiment with overlaying colour. But a vast range of colours is unnecessary and can, indeed, be confusing. Try using a range of large-nibbed pens in red, blue, orange, pink, green, violet and yellow. It is best to avoid black, as this can leave a heavy, almost 'dirty', effect.

Fibre-tips are also available in water-soluble varieties which can produce interesting effects when brushed with water.

Pastels

Pastels are powdered pigments mixed with gum or resin to form a rather dry paste which is then moulded into pastel sticks. Oil pastels differ in that the oil binding them makes them less brittle and fragile than pure pastel. There are now pastels on the market that work almost like crayons or paints, and are water-soluble, but nonetheless there are effectively only two main types of pastel. Most people start by indulging in a set of soft pastels, perhaps remembering the work of Degas, but oil pastels are probably easier to use. Both are effective when working for embroidery. Each type is used a little differently, so I will describe their use separately.

Soft pastels

These can be used a little like chalk or conté. Their willingness to smudge can be a problem, so control requires some practice. Areas can be fixed at any stage during the drawing process and then more colour or detail added, to avoid the image becoming a complete blur. Try underlying the final drawing with contrasting coolness and warmness of colour, or try underlying areas with complementary colour – these effects can be used to bring the pastel drawing alive.

Pastels can also be underlaid with watercolour, which may be used to define general areas of colour on the paper before pastels are added, or the pastel can be fixed and watercolour or gouache added at a later stage, and again more pastels added. This layering of colour and media will create a richer and more colourful effect than trying to draw with pastel in direct colours from the stick and just rubbing these out on to blank paper.

Oil pastels

Layers built up in oil pastel will mix well if not fixed in between. Oil pastels built up in thick layers will provide intensity of colour, although this can be quietened by adding layers of softer tints. Alternatively, oil pastels can be brushed out with turpentine if thinner layers of colour are desired. Try both methods and experiment with different papers. Both oil and soft pastels react differently on different textures: rough papers provide a 'key' and take off more colour, but a more even all-over effect is possible on smooth papers.

Oil pastels can also act as a resist for other media, so try them with water-based paints and crayons. Both types of pastel work well with other media for mixed media drawings, and can often rescue a painting that was just about to be given up.

Paint

There are many types of paint on the market and they are all better than the ones you used at school, and therefore you will inevitably achieve better results! Many people are terrified of paint and brushes, but there is really no need. Again, practising beforehand can increase confidence.

This sample shows marks that can be made with crayons, fibre-tips, soft pastels and oil pastels. Water has been added in places where the media would respond

The choice of paper is important if a good start is to be made. For best results try a 70 or 140 lb watercolour paper. This is available in 'rough' or 'not', according to whether texture or an accuracy in linework is required. There are many types which include both factory and handmade, and different grades of finish – do experiment, but for ease of choice, start with an ordinary rough factory-made paper.

If the paint is to be used fairly dry, a 140 lb paper will not need stretching, although this is always a wise precaution to prevent a rippled surface. Stretching paper sounds difficult, and everyone has a different method. Here is one that is incredibly simple, and it works.

Choose a drawing board about 3 cm (1½ in) bigger than the paper all around (or cut the paper to fit an available board). The drawing board should ideally be too thick to bend and not plastic faced (exterior quality 12 mm or ½ in plywood is ideal). Place the paper on the board, and cut four lengths of 5 cm (2 in) wide brown gummed paper, one for each side. With a medium-sized household paintbrush, brush water evenly over the surface of the paper. The thicker the paper, the more

will be required. Work in long strokes until the paper is evenly wet; do not touch it or try to smooth it out. Starting at a long side, wet the gummed paper (do this by dabbing the paintbrush along it; do not wipe the brush along in one stroke as too much gum will be removed). Place the gummed paper along a long edge of the paper, with about half of the gummed strip on the paper and half on the board (not over the edge of the board). Repeat the process on one of the shorter sides, then on the other two sides. Now stand the board up to dry, away from direct heat. Half-way through drying, turn the board up the other way. If the paper does split, simply repair the split with more gummed paper and use the remaining area. Any splits are usually near the tape anyway.

Now you need to consider which paints are going to be most useful, which colours to buy, and what paintbrushes to choose. The following types of paint are readily available: watercolour, gouache, acrylic and oil. I include a rough guide to their properties and usefulness, with suggestions for experiments which can be tried with all of them at the end of the section.

This notebook page shows the use of gouache in solid colour and washes, and experiments with different brushes and brush strokes

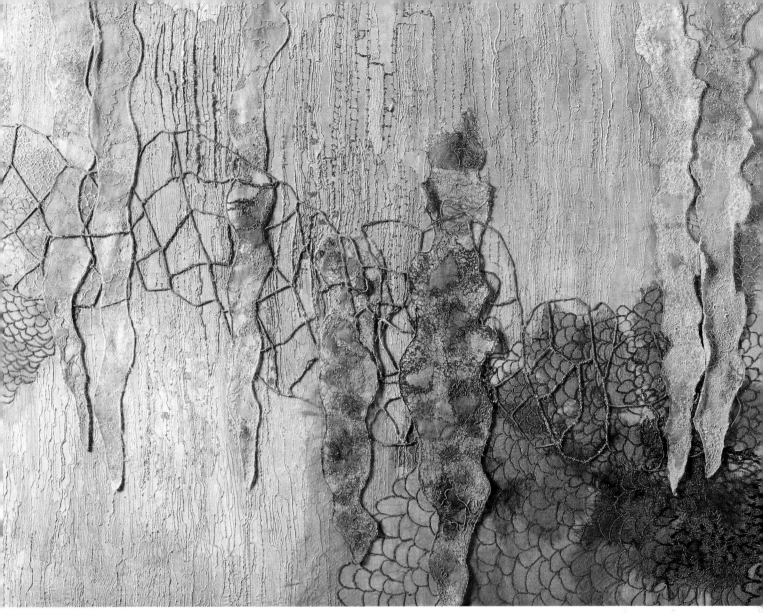

A personal view of wisteria. Worked on a dyed and machine embroidered background, with additional nets made on vanishing fabric. The free-hanging wisteria flowers are worked separately on organza edged with a whip-stitched cord (Roma Edge)

Watercolour

Watercolour is available in pans (solid pigment) or tubes (a more liquid form). For convenience, and especially for painting outside, pans in a tray are the most useful, but choose a good artist's quality so that they can easily be used.

Watercolour is essentially a transparent medium; that is, each layer of paint will not completely cover the preceding one, which will still affect the final layer in terms of colour and tonal value. This has an interesting quality for the embroiderer – images could be layered with see-through fabrics or scrims, straight stitches layered, or dyes used. The disadvantage is that mistakes cannot be covered over with additional pigments, although further detail can be added. The only way to disguise mistakes is to add another medium, which can be effective. Mixed media drawings offer a greater variety of mark to the embroiderer who is constantly looking for new ideas in relation to texture and colour mixing. Thus pastel (oil or soft), crayons and gouache can all be used to enhance watercolour paintings and provide additional information for embroideries, if not actually to win prizes in local watercolour competitions!

Gouache

Gouache paint is a designer's medium available in tubes and sometimes in pans. Gouache is a much denser medium than watercolour, with a higher saturation of pigment. It can be used for thin washes in a similar way to watercolour, and can also be used for intense opaque areas of colour. It is not as translucent as watercolour, but it is more versatile. This quality makes it a useful buy if the budget is limited. The following colours are recommended from series 1 (the cheaper range of colours): spectrum yellow, lemon yellow, spectrum red, alizarian crimson, bright green, violet, lamp black, zinc white and cobalt blue.

The same brushes can be used for gouache and watercolour. Student quality sable will be sufficient: choose a variety of sizes from 0 to 7. In addition, a haké brush or Japanese tapered brush may prove interesting.

The greater variety of mark and saturation of colour available with gouache is useful to the embroiderer, and it is also successful when used as part of a mixed media drawing.

Acrylic and oil paints

Acrylics are the modern, water-soluble equivalent to turpentine thinned oil paint. Each type of paint has its adherents who prefer the drying qualities of one, or the ease of application of the other. There are many additives that can be used to improve smoothness or texture, drying qualities (to slow down acrylic or to speed up oil), flexibility or whatever. Oils and acrylics can be fun. By supplying a surface that can be smooth or heavily textured, they offer intense colour and previous mistakes can be obliterated or removed if worked on a properly prepared surface. They can,

however, prove quite a task to master in themselves, so unless these methods of painting are to provide an additional hobby, it is best to steer clear of them.

Experiments for paint, brushes and papers

Try the following experiments with each of the paints on a variety of papers so that comparisons can be made. If only gouache is available, experiments in the one medium will still be useful to gain an understanding and build up confidence. First experiment with colour saturation. Slowly add more and more water or thinning medium to the paint and try to paint an evenly coloured square with each saturation. Next try grading tones of colour from dark to light. Do this by adding more water, then try to achieve good grading by adding white pigment. Paint can also be 'brushed out' by adding colour then wiping it away with a brush that is kept clean and a little wet – keep a rag or tissue handy to remove excess water and pigment from the brush.

Next, try layering thin washes of the same colour, then thin washes of different colours, allowing the paper to dry between washes. Try a thin wash over

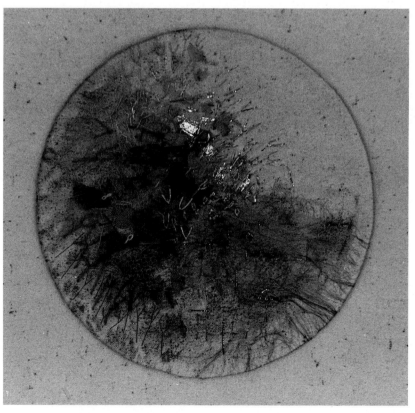

This embroidery, worked direct from life, is of aubretia tumbling over a Cotswold stone wall. The dyeing is done with fibre-tip dyes, then layers of chiffon are added, with a reserved approach to hand stitching in a variety of threads (Roma Edge)

Worked directly from the Red Garden at Hidcote Manor, Gloucestershire. The fabrics and papers were placed on the background in the garden and some hand stitches added. Additional machine embroidery was worked on return to the studio (by the author)

thick paint – this can be useful to add tonal values, but do it quickly to avoid taking up the first layer of paint.

Now see how textured you can make your results. Try the paint on different papers, including handmade. Try using different thicknesses of paint and applying it with unorthodox implements – as well as knives and spatulas, try straws, bits of rag, sponge, dipped thread and so on. Try painting on coloured surfaces, such as newspaper or magazines chopped up and layered with the paint.

Now experiment with the brushes. How thin a line can each one draw? How thick? What happens if the brush is dabbed? With wet paint? With dry paint? Can straight lines be made with long continuous strokes? Can such a line be changed from thick to thin? Or change direction? Try using different brushes and different thicknesses of paint.

Keep all experiments in a notebook which can be taken into the garden as a reference, just like a stitch reference book! Gradually a vocabulary of marks and techniques will be built up so that painting too can be approached with confidence.

When starting out it is often difficult to decide which media to purchase – just how much is needed? Rather than buying a little of everything, it is important to have enough colours of a good quality product in anything that is chosen. A good artist's suppliers will advise on the best brands to buy.

Pencils will prove essential, and are useful for sketchbook work (a sketchbook should be carried at all times!). Colour media are necessary, and unfortunately are usually expensive. A box of ten gouache tubes is available from most manufacturers and this can be a useful starting point – although you will also need brushes. If working in paint seems a little daunting, a good set of crayons may seem more economical as brushes will then not be essential and work can be done on cartridge paper rather than stretched or watercolour paper. If either of these is chosen as the basic tool, additional media can be acquired when necessary. Each medium will have its own benefits and restrictions; by becoming aware of these through practice and familiarity it will be possible to gauge which new media should be added to the collection in order to achieve new possibilities and effects. Gradually, a personal collection of suitable media will be built up, all of which will be useful.

Mark-making and colour notes in textile media

It is usual to see paper as one whole piece, or fabrics and threads only in the sewing room, and these media are too rarely experimented with. Working directly with textiles can, however, be very rewarding, particularly if you are nervous of the more traditional art media. Mark-making or drawing using more familiar materials can be a way into observing from life that is not daunting yet does create original results. Eyes can be opened and surroundings fully observed in an effort to distil the necessary information on colour, light, shade, and texture – all lessons that will eventually help when working with artist's material is finally attempted. Even for someone who is used to artist's materials, the change to working directly in textiles can offer genuinely exciting results.

To begin, take a collection of things into the garden: dyes (fibre-tip dyes are the easiest to use in this instance), a piece of fabric in a ring or on a small square frame (bear in mind that the finished embroidery will almost inevitably turn out the size and shape of the frame on which the fabric is mounted), a variety of threads, coloured papers and fabrics (consider textures), and also basic sewing equipment. Choose an area of garden, decide why you have chosen it and distil this thought into a few words on which to concentrate as the work proceeds. Is the work to be about patterns? The simplicity of a few colours? The muddle of texture and colour? Is the area light and airy or dark and damp? Is it autumnal or summery? Cold or warm? By thinking this through as the image is composed, the work will benefit and become coherent in its theme.

It may help to eliminate the blankness of the fabric as soon as possible, so make a few dyed marks, or cut up fabrics and papers and attach them with pins or stitches. Now things have started, they will develop quickly. It is possible to unpick anything that does not work, but don't be too quick to do so. Always try to establish why something is unsuccessful first, or the same mistake may be made again.

Through the careful consideration of the marks made and the colours and textures added, whether through layering paper, fabric, stitches, dyes or a collection of all of these, it is possible to complete a small piece in a day of careful observation.

The final piece may often be a starting point for a new way of working – new methods are often tried in a desperate attempt to relate to a part of nature. The piece of embroidery may provide the source material for a worksheet or an idea for a larger piece of work, or collection of pieces. Sometimes work arising from this method is very free in approach, sometimes it is very formal, and perhaps suited for a repeat motif on a garment or piece of household furnishing, but the work itself is never boring!

2

APPROACHING THE SUBJECT

*'The mixing of colours and the variety of brush and brush stroke
are discussed as a means towards representation of the spirit
of the object and of the scene as a whole – for instance, in painting the
doorway to a garden, one's aim should be to indicate the quality
of tranquillity and isolation such a doorway implies. Likewise trees
should illustrate the qualities that such plants embody.'*
Chieh Tzu Yuan Hua Chuan, *The Tao of Painting*, 1679

THE choice of subject matter is important for anyone new to painting and drawing. Eventually the process of drawing will seem so stimulating in itself that very simple or apparently boring objects will attract attention and offer subjects of interest. At first, however, it is a good idea to find a subject or view that will be sufficiently interesting that any lack of confidence or drawing skill will become submerged as the qualities of the subject take over the drawing.

Gardens are an excellent subject for embroidery, and a very useful starting point when trying to learn more about art materials and mark-making. Within one garden, or indeed one view, there may be inspiration for practising working in monochrome or colour; for creating depth or form; or for using perspective.

Choosing a suitable garden to draw will have a lot to do with the sort of medium that is to be used and the kind of drawing practice that is intended.

For initial tonal drawings, find a small area of garden with variety in leaf or flower shapes, and that is in a good light so that contrasts of light and shade are created.

When working in colour for the first time find an area of a border with a variety of plants and a great deal of colour variation. Avoid areas where leaves predominate, as too much green may be difficult to observe initially – the subtle nuances required to make such an area work will take some practice. Instead, choose a wide selection of colour in closely-packed flower forms.

As progress is made and skills improve, composition will become important, and tonal, textural and colour information will play a supporting role. Even if the drawing is only about colour or a collection of plant shapes, it should be composed for the best effect, as good composition will make even the most ordinary collection of marks seem more interesting.

The placement of blocks and quantities of colour or tonal values within the work can affect composition and add weight or lightness to the overall feeling of the picture. As skills develop, other forms can be included such as pots of flowers, shrubs, steps, trees or large foreground flowers. The inclusion of any such objects must be done with care: a large structure can be very distracting if placed in the centre of a composition, unless it is well supported by other formal qualities. Experiment with the positioning of structures and forms to create satisfactory compositions that rely on

This view would make a good starting point for a drawing concentrating on tonal values or shape. From Le Parc des Moutiers, Verangeville-sur-Mer, France

Hostas make an excellent source for tonal drawings when a little experience has been gained. From Le Parc des Moutiers

symmetrical and asymmetrical formats. Singular structures of pots, shrubs, gates, trees and so on can be placed at the side of the picture to lead the eye in, but as this device can be a little obvious, it should be handled with care.

Line is important to a composition. Although drawings of gardens may contain few straight lines, linear qualities may begin to emerge. Drawings of tall stemmed flowers will stress the vertical; areas of ground cover will tend to emphasise the horizontal; areas of paving or lawn leading into the garden will create diagonals.

It is important to recognise the ideas and feelings that can be expressed by including different types of line. Vertical lines can emphasise the growing nature of a garden and, by using a low horizon in an image of mostly vertical lines, this impression of reaching upwards can be increased.

Including a greater number of horizontal lines in a composition will add to the sense of horizon, and give an earthbound quality to the picture. Structures will be flattened and the sense of earth and weightiness will be stronger. The effect is far from dynamic, but instead feels rather heavy, although it can have an air of reassurance.

Diagonal lines incorporated into a composition will give a sense of depth as they are often used to indicate perspective, and this will occur even if the diagonals are only stems of flowers. Diagonal lines will also impart a sense of dynamism to the picture, making the final result seem more exciting or, if overdone, muddled and agitated. The intensity of such a drawing can be increased with mixtures of clashing colour or interrupted marks – such intensity and movement makes an interesting starting point for an embroidery.

Organising all these elements within a drawing can help to build up an understanding of composition and the compositional possibilities of line and linear qualities. Choosing tonal or colour values in relation to this composition will also increase this awareness, and embroideries worked with such knowledge will be more confident in their effect. It will become possible to know why something works instead of accepting a happy accident.

Creating a balanced composition can be more difficult than it sounds at first. It will be necessary to attract the eye's attention by some device – a focal point or a means of leading the eye into the picture. Having attracted attention, there must be enough interest to keep the eye, and no easy line of escape. For example, a path which leads to a tree but which then goes directly out of the paper at the top of the path will be very unsuccessful. Balance, although not necessarily an even balance – it can be deliberately one-sided – will need to be effected by weights of colour or tone and by setting out the main objects of interest. Be wary of compositions that have an exact symmetrical quality unless you want to make sure the eye is led directly to a focal point. Although such an image can seem very charming initially, it will need a good central focus to sustain interest. Practise with balanced and imbalanced compositions, testing weights of different objects, colours, tones and textures against each other. Compositions that seem imbalanced structurally can be successful if a balance is restored through the use of weights of colour or tone.

When looking at embroidery, people are often so fascinated by the variety of stitches or techniques that has been used that their attention is held even if the composition or planning of the work is not so good. In painting and drawing these devices are not available, so painting must initially win interest from a good understanding of composition. This understanding will of course pay dividends when applied to embroidery, which will stand as a result in its own right as a good composition from a distance, as well as holding interest as a fascinating collection of stitches, colours or techniques when viewed more closely.

Acquiring an eye for composition can take some practice, so experiment with moving around compositional elements on worksheets. It will also help considerably to look at the paintings of other artists. Artists in the Renaissance experimented considerably with composition, and devices such as dividing the picture plane into what were considered to be perfect proportions, the use of diagonals to point to important features or to give a sense of depth or dynamism, or a heightened sense of the vertical to indicate the presence of God are all prevalent. In later landscape painting the use of horizontals and verticals imparts mood to a landscape, giving either an heroic or a romantic notion, according to their proportions. In Impressionist and Post-Impressionist painting, in addition to an informed sense of colour, there are compositions that suggest approaches to gardens. These artists worked a great deal with natural light and colour. Their paintings were usually done outdoors and often in gardens, and they had a sense of composition that was informed by the new invention of the camera – giving the feeling that the image might continue outside the immediate picture plane. Because of photography, their compositions were also less rigid, less symmetrical and less obviously contrasted with devices to lead the eye and so forth. Although such devices can be useful, today's preference seems to be for greater subtlety.

Looking at the work of such artists can help, but how can this be applied to drawing, painting and mark-making records, and eventually to the final embroidery?

When faced with a large area of garden, a beautiful extended border, or a large collection of leafy shrubs, it can be hard to decide what to draw and, further, to attend to exactly what has been chosen. There is a tendency to draw a view that extends for 180 degrees to the extremes of vision. This should be resisted as, apart from being far too much to tackle successfully, the result will almost certainly be repetitive and monotonous, as well as creating a boring composition. Such a view, if cut down, would provide adequate information as well as making a better drawing. The fact that there would be less content would ensure that details were observed more closely.

Many people who take superbly composed photographs find composition in drawing and painting as difficult as do those without photographic experience, but devising a good composition is easier if the lessons learned from photography are employed. The easiest way to find a good composition from views that present themselves, and to develop an eye for composition, is to use a viewfinder. A viewfinder can be made in one of two ways, and can then be looked through in order to compose the picture.

Perhaps the simplest way of making a viewfinder, and the best for a novice, is to cut a hole in a stiff piece of paper. If a number of shapes are made, these can be moved close to the eye or further away to change the amount of the view that can be seen. Lines made on the viewfinder will help to indicate where certain features should occur in the drawing.

The other method is to cut two pieces of stiff card into L-shapes of about 15–20 cm (6–8 in) with sides 8 cm ($3\frac{1}{2}$ in) wide. These can be used to make any size and shape when in front of a view. This is a good method of composing a drawing when a little experienced. The fact that the view can be altered so easily can prove too tempting for novices, who may

Cottage-style borders are ideal for colour drawings. Take a low viewpoint – try sitting on the ground for the painting. View in Ilmington, Warwickshire

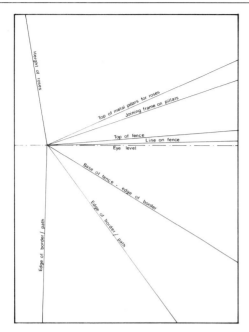

The diagonals offered by the perspective in this image give the picture a sense of dynamism, of going somewhere, of excitement. The eye level is worked out from available information – the angles of the lines seen and where they converge. Then the lines representing the edges of things can be drawn to a vanishing point on this eye level. The resulting information can be used as a starting point for a drawing or embroidery

Tonal drawing where the lines of the perspective are reintroduced, the verticals are given a stronger role, and the lilies are simplified to become triangles. The trees are formalised and included in the composition. Tonal values are then worked out from the original drawing. Textures are evolved, including a texture for the gravel path

Pen drawing at Giverny. The diagonals of the perspective are further aided in the final drawing by the diagonals of the lilies in the foreground. The strong tones in the foreground and distance, with the softer tones in the middle distance, give a sense of depth. The negative shapes expressed through the application of heavy shadow, and created by the lilies in the foreground, as well as the path which is left blank, are all important to the composition – at least as important as the drawn shapes themselves. The vertical lines increase the sense of something growing. The almost horizontal hedge offers a strong horizon and sense of earth. The trees behind the fence were left out for reasons of clarity

The weights of tonal values are reversed in this drawing. The heavier tones are now concentrated towards the base of the picture, and this imparts a weightiness to the whole image. The dark triangular shapes of the lilies brings them into the foreground of the picture. The sense of distance is aided, not only by the lines of perspective, but also by the softer shading of the trees which appear higher and further away, and because of the lily covering the vanishing point which causes a feeling that this view goes on for ever

Wisteria worked by machine using a zigzag stitch of varying widths on coloured soft scrim (by the author)

find that they are once again trying to draw everything that can be seen.

At first look for interesting shapes, tonal or textural qualities or colours, and gradually add form and depth to the drawings. Formal ornamentation associated with gardens can also be added as confidence is gained. Pots with flowers, doorways, archways, trees, statues, steps, ponds, topiary, paths, hedges, seats and so on all make interesting additions to gardens, and will lend a focus to drawings and embroideries.

Many garden features can be used to frame the drawing, obviating the necessity to look constantly through a viewfinder. Try drawing such frames in monochrome at first, as it may be easier to handle the depths, light, shade and perspective problems created in pencil before going on to work in colour. Many frames are fairly obvious – looking through an open doorway or window can be very straightforward, and these can be particularly interesting, especially if a window-sill or foreground interest is incorporated in the view. This

could be noticeably manmade as a point of contrast to the nature beyond; or plants and flowers featured in the foreground can allow the close study of plant forms against the more general background. This can be very successful as a drawing exercise, and useful for an embroidery where the foreground could be worked in three dimensions to really bring the view to life.

Many gardens have entrances that will frame a view, archways, doorways in outside walls, openings in hedges and so on, but frames can be found that are much more subtle. Trees may form a strong natural arch; a particularly strong form in a flower may create a natural framing at one or two sides of the picture; walls, or a corner where two walls meet, may offer a structure for a frame; trellises, canes in allotments, edges of patios or ponds can all offer scope for framing ideas. Frames form a useful study area for embroidery, as problems often arise when an original method of presenting the work is sought. If the original drawing already has its own 'frame', the problem of finishing

This embroidery relates in its way of portraying gardens to the drawings on the right of page 34. Colour and more textural marks are also attended to. Fabrics are laid on to a surface to indicate broad sweeps of colour. These are then stitched into by hand and machine. The 'patchwork' effect is maintained, although the stitching gradually merges some areas

the embroidery may be practically solved. The frame can be embroidered and the central embroidery placed within it.

A useful device to add interest to your drawing and embroidery is to include something which leads into the picture. This can give qualities of depth as well as ensuring that the eye, and with it the interest of the viewer, is taken into the picture. Paths are the obvious answer, but lawn edges, steps, encroaching walls, trellises, rows of trees or topiary, or a collection of similar shapes or colours can all lead to a focal point in the picture plane, if not actually into the garden itself. This last device can be particularly helpful in an herbaceous border, which may otherwise have a strip-like quality. A strong shape or area of colour to one side of the image will also prevent the eye from leaving the image too quickly.

When using garden features to lead the eye into the picture, try to include a point of interest. Try looking down a path at a focal point – a statue or fountain, a bench or gazebo, a pot of flowers or a weeping tree, a couple or a single person. The focal point will give the image a story or perhaps a feeling of rest or solitude, the idea of a secret garden, or a garden of secrets. For a central feature, a weeping tree is preferable to an upright one (which leads the eye out of the picture).

An entrance can act as a sort of welcome into the picture, so an open door or gate, an archway or a path will all help to give a feeling of friendliness to the drawing or embroidery and increase the desire of the viewer to stay.

Whether the picture contains descriptions of garden forms or is simply a mass of tone, colour or texture, there should be variety in the qualities of intensity. Areas of texture should be varied, heavily worked details or areas contrasted with spaces of simple tone and little or no texture. Try to create contrast when using shape or form – choose different leaf shapes for contrast and try manipulating them in front of shadow or a brightly lit wall or paved area. To create interest and balance, contrast areas of high activity with areas of little or no activity – remember, blank spaces and negative shapes are as important as the areas of interest and detail.

Colours should be carefully chosen, as the picture will be more satisfying if the colours are harmonious (close together on the colour wheel) or if sets of complementaries are used (opposite sides on the colour wheel). There are many who insist that the use of colour, and our likes and dislikes, is subjective, but this is not the case. If a colour scheme is attractive or displeasing there is usually an objective or scientific reason for this. Most human eyes respond to colour in the same or similar ways, so responses to clash, contrast and harmony will always be more or less the same. If this is borne in mind when choosing an area to draw, the end result is more likely to conform to the mood or notion required.

An archway of hedging reveals a path leading through a topiaried garden to a pool and an enclosed garden beyond at Hidcote Manor in Gloucestershire. The composition has a slightly off-centre focal point. The simple marks build up to give changes in light and shade: these marks could easily be translated into hand or machine stitching

As progress is made with looking at and understanding the subject, and with using artists' materials, the views chosen can become more unusual or ambitious. Remember that bright light will make a subject come alive, and will define colours and tones well. Unfortunately, bright light has a tendency to change frequently, so drawings will have to be completed more quickly, or you will have to use the Impressionist technique of starting one painting, then going on to another when the light has changed too much, and then to another. If this process is continued over a number of days until all the paintings are finished, the collection will show a valuable study of light – as do Monet's *Cathedral* paintings.

Composition is best explored in a garden with many

The interesting shapes and textures of the plant forms in this area of garden at Barnsley House, Gloucestershire, make it an excellent subject for a monochrome drawing. Shape, texture, or tone could each be studied, and the carved stonework provides an excellent off-centre focal point

Often, when recording information for embroidery, there may be considerations other than the production of a good composition. The drawing may be required to provide informed studies which bear a relationship to gardens, but which are essentially records of colour, texture, shape or pattern. These may be useful and inspiring for a whole range of textile experiments and embroideries that are not merely pictorial. In such cases, composition, and even contrast, may be of less value, but still bear in mind that the final paperwork will be more useful if, in addition to being well observed rather than sheer invention, there are also variations in the intensity of the different qualities of tone, colour, mark, texture and so on. The subject matter should be suitable to provide this contrast for the choice of medium, and the medium should be suitable for the sort of textile investigation that is to follow. It would obviously be unsuitable to use pencils if a colour study was required for patchwork, or watercolours if a highly textured piece was needed for stitch experiments.

This embroidery, worked in relief, uses the door and doorway to frame a courtyard garden. The foreground interest brings the garden out to meet the viewer, and offers a welcome into the garden. Various stumpwork methods were used for this piece. The leaves are worked with needleweaving over wire; the inner door and window are padded satin stitch; the pots under the window are padded silk; the flowers in the pot by the door are worked with needlemade lace in a tailor's buttonhole stitch and raised from the first surface stitches; the table and chair are constructed on card, as is the door frame; the rug is a canvas work slip; the paving, stones, step and foreground pot are card and wood covered in silk; the dandelions are tufted stranded cotton; and the dandelion leaves and foot scraper are needlemade lace over wire (Janet Bramwell)

features, and it will be easiest if the garden is made up of small composed areas rather than long views with undulating countryside, so try a garden like Hidcote in Gloucestershire, or Sissinghurst in Kent.

For considering colour it is not necessary, once experience is gained, to choose a view with a lot of colours. Shades of one or two colours will give practice in the subtle mixing of paint or pastel. There are many gardens set out in single colour schemes. At Hidcote Manor there is a red garden which is particularly good for experimenting with colour mixing – testing for every shade of red from fiery red/orange to red/violet, then mixing greens from bright lime to brown/green and through to red again in *Cordyline* species. In my own garden I have created a border which has only blue violets contrasted against yellow; the only other colours are provided by the leaves, many of which are grey/green or silver, to provide a breathing space for the complementaries.

If you experiment with both looking (really looking!) and mark-making, in time choosing a view that is useful and informative will become easy. But do not let the search for the elusive perfect view prevent an early start on a drawing. Choose a garden, find a view that has enough interest, and start. If a preferable view is found later, it can always be returned to another time. Starting a drawing or painting is almost as difficult as deciding when it is finished, but the more often it is done, the easier it will become.

Experience with drawing and embroidery may make the translation from one to the other easier, and in fact can often make this process too easy, so that a drawing in a certain style or medium seems to automatically suggest a certain type of embroidery. At the drawing stage it is best not to be concerned about the finished piece of work. Even if a specific project is envisaged, it is better to do many drawings and then select from them, rather than to draw a certain subject for a certain result – although this may become part of the worksheet process. If a drawing is undertaken with a strict brief for the ensuing embroidery, it is likely that both the preliminary work and the embroidery will turn out stilted, uninteresting and obvious in conception. An example is the person determined to do some quilting who therefore sets out to draw a stone wall for that purpose. If the subject is approached with an open mind, other sources for quilting may emerge simply from the drawing style adopted (the use of monochrome, particularly in fibre-tips, might be useful in this instance, as may any line drawing, perhaps with

LEFT: **Courtyard with bougainvillea at the Thermal Springs on Rhodes.** Worked on dyed, felted silk wadding with chiffons and machine stitching (by the author)

The trunk of this wisteria offers an excellent frame to the side and top of the picture. The branches and the tall onion spires lead to the sculpture as the focal point in this picture. Barnsley House, Gloucestershire

a wash). If the embroiderer is determined to work a stone wall, then other techniques such as dyeing, layering fabrics, machine or hand stitchery, canvas work, cut work, reverse appliqué, even vanishing fabric layers, suggest themselves. The list is endless and the opportunity for experimentation and sampling from informed drawing is immense – so do keep an open mind!

In order to concentrate on the drawing or painting instead of on the final embroidery, which could so easily narrow responses to the image, consider only the garden. Decide what it is that is especially interesting about the view. Is it the colours? The textures? The mood of the garden? Its apparent or real coolness or warmth? Its verdant quality? Is it the collection of shapes in a leafy glade? The formality of the layout? The quality of light? The muddle or orderliness? Try to decide precisely what is the essence of the garden that attracts the attention, and formulate this into a word or two which describe these feelings. The word or words can then be concentrated on whilst drawing and

This painting represents the whole experience of visiting Hidcote Manor Gardens in Gloucestershire. The view does not actually exist, but is rather culled from a number of images and views in the garden. The final result sums up one person's idea of a particular garden. Worked in acrylic paint and some oil pastel, the pencil marks around the outside were added later and the whole piece became a starting point for the colour photograph in the frontispiece (Marilyn Phipps)

The fruit trees and path guide the eye to the off-centre focal point of the chair surrounded by trellising

may also be used to affect the final embroidery and add qualities of mood or an experience to the work, rather than the embroidery being just a collection of colours, textures, techniques or patterns.

Choosing the most suitable medium or mixture of media is essential to a successful piece of work so, having decided on a particular aspect of the garden, this is the next consideration, unless the view was chosen for an exercise in a specific medium.

Shape and form can be expressed simply by using line and tone, and it may not be necessary to include colour unless it is interesting and vital to the image. An effective embroidery can be worked in monochrome, so do consider this.

Two drawings of a view, one which concentrates on shape, form and light and shade, and one which is solely concerned with colour, could be useful, especially if inexperience makes these aspects difficult to combine. Both drawings could be used for an interesting series of embroideries, perhaps concentrating on different techniques, and including different responses to colour, amounts of texture and so on.

Drawings purely of colour areas and their relationships can be quite expressive, but with some practice consideration can also be given to textural qualities. Depth and form can be expressed by using complementaries or warmer and cooler colours.

The mood of a garden, its formality or informality, its calmness or busyness or whether it has a feeling of agitation or relaxation, can all be expressed in either monochrome or colour. By experimenting with collections of marks, ways of treating these various qualities will be found that are personal and unique, and will in turn offer a mark of individuality to future embroidery.

Different media can create their own responses. Charcoal can be used to express heaviness – perhaps a garden before a storm, or an area left to run wild.

Watercolours and gouache used in thin transparent layers can be used to indicate the coolness of water gardens, as well as their actual appearance. The possibilities of mixing and layering with paint makes it suitable for any area with a high density of colour, and acrylic paint can portray excitement, agitation or confusion if its qualities of layering and textural build-up are used.

A sense of calm can be expressed by gentler additions of paint, pastel or crayon. This feeling can be aided by eliminating black from the drawing – adding blues and violets to the colours that are used to give depth and shade to the drawing.

A feeling of sunlight and lightness of mood can be achieved with thinly layered paint, or using soft pastels in layers or over paint. This quality will be increased by adding yellow to areas of intense sunlight, and by lightening colours by adding yellow rather than just white.

The agitation of an image, or the feeling of excitement or confusion will be increased by using mixed media or layers of heavily worked pastel or acrylic. Papers can be added to drawings or bits and pieces of garden material included for texture. Conflicting line and clashing colour will increase the sense of agitation, and contrasting colour quantities will also help – for example, red 'spots' of flowers on a green ground will increase excitement because of the 'jumping' effect these complementaries have on the eye if used in this way.

Experimentation with these effects on the 'mood' of a drawing will be rewarding for the drawing and the embroideries which follow. The garden view will inform the picture, and the words, thoughts and application of the media will concentrate its expressive content.

Although an open mind must be maintained as to the nature of the finished embroidery, it is important to remember that the drawings and paintings are by an embroiderer for embroidery. Thus the most important consideration is to capture the qualities of the garden that will be important and relevant to building up an understanding in order for the final work to be

Watercolour and gouache painting with oil pastels of ceonothus and foreground flowers in Le Parc des Moutiers. The blue weeping quality of the ceonothus becomes the main body of the drawing. Textures are added with gouache and oil pastel (by the author)

undertaken. The paperwork will not necessarily be judged as a piece of artwork in its own right, but rather as a preparatory piece for something else. Every effort must be made to produce the best piece of work possible, so concentrate fully on the task, although this may be difficult at first. The most important criteria for the paperwork is that it be useful and informative, and supply inspiration for future work. It is this that will mark it out as a success or failure. Keep working on one image, and if it starts to go amiss, work on the same view on another piece of paper in a different medium to gain a different set of information and a better understanding of the subject. After a while it will be possible to return with confidence to the original drawing or painting and work further on that.

As well as remembering to regard things as an embroiderer instead of as an artist, resist the temptation to look at the subject through the eyes of a gardener. Experience with gardens may certainly help in the choice of an interesting view for the drawing,

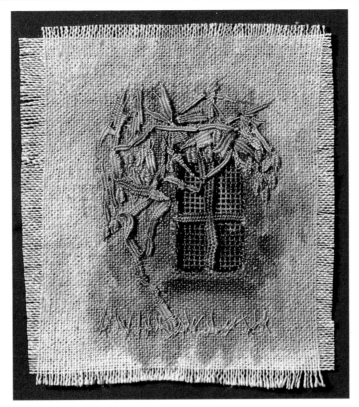

A small sample. Wisteria worked in needleweaving on a dyed ground cut for a window (Eileen Bissell)

but at this point stop being a gardener. For an embroiderer, a drawing or painting must capture a set of colours and textures, perhaps describe form and depth, and hopefully, create a mood; rarely will it be necessary to explain exquisite botanical detail. The drawings, and, correspondingly, the embroidery, will be freer, more experimental and perhaps more abstract, or, what is often surprising, seemingly more lifelike, if a knowledge of plant and flower types is not allowed to interfere with the drawing. Instead of thinking about drawing lavender, for instance, consider it as a collection of small mauve blobs or strokes placed haphazardly on grey/green lines. With a little imagination, all plants and flowers will become a collection of different marks, colours and tones instead of an individually drawn and fussed-over flower. The drawing will thus become more suitable as a starting point for embroidery, which is often in itself a collection of colours and marks. This approach will be easier and less frustrating for the novice getting to grips with new

LEFT: **Entrance to a garden**. The dyed ground is worked on a wax resist. The embroidery is worked by machine. The arched doorway and path are quilted and mounted separately on the garden background, giving a sense of depth. The wisteria on the wall shows another way of working this flower (Sian Kibblewhite)

The sunlight through the laburnum tree, against a heavier tree in the background is captured in this quick pastel sketch. Each mark and scribble or block of colour represents a flower or plant form. The tree is under-planted with a mass of onion flowers; the stems and leaves form a muddle of lines stroked down quickly onto a cream-coloured paper ground (by the author)

materials and working on paper.

When starting to draw from subject matter for the first time, remember the notes and experiments from Chapter 1. Notebooks could even be taken on drawing trips for information and further experiments if this should prove necessary. The marks that have been experienced in embroidery may also prove useful when creating marks in drawings.

Different media can be combined for added interest and texture, or if a satisfactory finish or mark cannot be obtained in one medium, and practising in a separate notebook is not helping, adding another medium to the work may help to overcome a particular hurdle. The mixture of media will also speak volumes when the drawings are translated into embroidery and textiles.

Once a drawing or painting is started, work on it until it is complete. It may be necessary to break off for additional sampling of marks, or because the light changes too drastically, or to work another sketch or drawing in a different medium to support and help the first; but always keep in mind the first drawing and complete it. Far more will be learned from finishing one drawing, no matter how tortuous the work feels, or how awful the drawing appears to be, than by stopping and starting afresh every time something seems to be going wrong. Remember that really looking, and thus understanding the subject, is the key to everything.

If the drawing does seem to be going badly, keep going and try to do as well as possible. The first few marks often look unpromising, or a lapse of concentration may cause a mistake to be made later on, but a drawing will look better as it is worked, and even something that looks like a failure on the surface can prove to be useful, perhaps through what has been learned, because the drawing does finally come together, or because there is a small part of the drawing that is successful and inspires some textile work.

A sense of achievement will be felt when an original piece of paperwork is completed that inspires a new and different approach to embroidery, or forms the starting point for a major piece of work. So many ideas may flood in when looking at the paperwork that it will be hard to know where to start. Conversely, the drawing or painting may be interesting, but may offer no concrete ideas for translation into embroidery. Even if only one idea presents itself, rather than diving straight into embroidery, this too should be checked and sampled. Whichever is the case, it is at this point that ideas should be really sorted out on paper. A little work on worksheets and sampling now will save a lot of disappointment later. Chapter 6 concentrates on the important, and often skipped over, process of worksheeting and sampling.

It is necessary to aim to make the most of the drawings and paintings so that a wide variety of ideas will present themselves for investigation. Whether drawing in monochrome or colour, using pattern, texture, line or form or combinations of these things, there are rules to be followed and rules to be broken, and this accumulated knowledge will, with some practice, give rewards and benefits in the ensuing embroidery. Even a complete beginner can bring a freshness and liveliness to drawing and a new approach to embroidery if a big enough effort is made.

So, having understood some of the basics about the media and a little about approaches to the subject, let us enter the garden.

Pen sketch of a gate to a wild garden, from a walled garden

3

TEXTURE AND TONE IN MONOCHROME

'Certain proportions of line, the combination of certain tones from the scale of tonal values . . . carry with them . . . quite distinctive and outstanding modes of expression.'

Paul Klee in a treatise *On Modern Art*, 1924

GARDENS offer an accessible source of inspiration for drawing in both monochrome and colour. Having experimented and become familiar with the media, it is now time to try recording a garden from life. Although monochromatic drawings will not offer the colour information that may be required for some embroideries, sketching in pen or pencil can seem less intimidating at first than using colour media. For colour information, make notes in pencil crayon at the side of the drawing (a good way to gradually become used to colour), or take good colour photographs. Even better is to use pen and pencil drawings for monochromatic embroideries or for additional information for colour drawings on texture and perspective.

A good place to start these first drawings is by recording line, pattern and shape. It will be easier if tone and form are ignored initially. Line drawing simply concerns itself with the description of outlines – although these can be affected by changes in pressure or thickness to indicate light and shade or distance from the viewer. Shape is simply the outline of the object. As collections of 'positive' shapes are drawn, the 'negative' shapes of the spaces in between will also become important to the drawing. Pattern can begin to occur as shapes repeat themselves against other shapes.

Texture may become important as a pattern emerges, or the strong use of tonal values may bring a pattern alive.

Finding a suitable subject is essential, so look for a variety of well-lit, clearly defined shapes, but check the sun as it will be difficult if the light changes drastically whilst the subject is being drawn. Drawing in monochrome will be easiest if there is not too much colour to cause confusion – at least initially, so keep the variety of colour to a minimum by choosing mainly leaf forms. Walls with climbers; hostas or lady's mantle or other leaf forms against walls; a good mix of ground cover plants or a crowded alpine garden or rockery; all will provide useful subject matter for monochrome.

Now look carefully at the subject and decide which way up the paper should be. This will be easy if the subject is being viewed through a viewfinder; otherwise, the choice must be made with care. If the feeling of the subject is tall and growing, with mainly vertical shapes and marks, a horizontal rectangle would make these lines feel squashed and shortened as the paper and the drawing fail to 'fit' each other. If the paper is used upright, the feeling of the vertical lines and the qualities of growth can be fully explored. If the subject is a long, horizontal image of plants tumbling over a wall, or flattish ground-cover plants, any

These paintings include additions of torn papers, and pencil marks (Fiona Purcell, while a student at Manchester Polytechnic)

attempt to fill a tall narrow piece of paper will be frustrating. The horizontality of the image and the way it clings to the earth will be best described on a horizontal rectangle of paper. All this sounds a little obvious, but in reality the case is rarely clear cut, and the question must be addressed seriously if the drawing is to be a success.

Now select a medium – a favourite pencil is a good idea to start. Choose a fairly soft one and keep it well sharpened, as line drawings look better if they are crisp rather than fuzzy – the inevitable result with a worn-down pencil. Do not be tempted to use an eraser as an answer to inadequate observation. The notion that any mistakes can be easily erased is likely to mean that more lines will be erased than left in place. So at

this stage only use an eraser as a last resort.

If the drawing appears to lack commitment, try changing the scale and medium. It is tempting to choose a small piece of paper when first using a pencil (perhaps thinking that any mistakes will also be small!), but this tends to cause the marks made to be more like writing than drawing as the pencil is manoeuvred by moving only the fingers, or, at best, the wrist. This can be eliminated by using a larger piece of paper, softer pencils, charcoal or thick fibre-tip pens.

Initially the pencil marks will look very even. This is all right as long as the subject is accurately observed, but as progress is made, and the exercises undertaken are brought into play, the thickness or strength of the line should reflect the quality of light or shade on that line, or its relationship to other elements in the picture plane – whether it is closer or further away. Things will appear distant if they are drawn fainter as they recede.

Try increasing the tonal range available by using a

The position adopted for drawing is important. The paper should be on a hard surface and kept as vertical as possible. The effects of foreshortening will make a drawing done on a horizontal board seem distorted when looked at straight on.

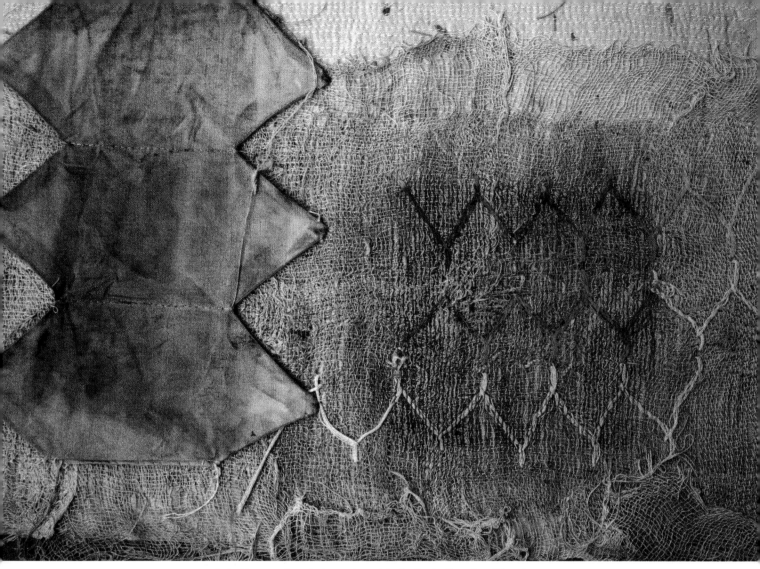

Embroidery sample worked on scrim and dyed cotton by Fiona Purcell from her paintings while a student at Manchester Polytechnic

variety of pressures with the pencil. Start by working with three different tones or pressures and work up to an infinite number. Try a line drawing where the shape of each leaf is carefully considered as well as its relationship to its neighbours. Make a palette of the types of marks that are to be used at the side of the drawing, so that comparisons can be made as the drawing carefully progresses.

The same drawing could be tried choosing one tonal value for each leaf. Each leaf would be filled in with its own tone, which would set it apart from its neighbours.

Finally, allow each leaf to take on as many tonal values as required to describe its form fully. It will be seen how much more adequately this describes the view, although the exercises may prove useful for embroidery as well as learning drawing.

A good line drawing will contain a variety of elements: different thicknesses of line and different intensities of mark – some heavily worked areas, some

places where one or two marks may define what is happening on quite a large expanse of paper. The drawing may indicate different qualities of texture as well as light and shade, and a depth of field can also be indicated by the use of softer, paler lines in the distance.

Distance can also be indicated by the intensity of texture. Objects in the foreground will be seen in more detail, and the closeness of the lines chosen will intensify this area against a less detailed distance. Alternatively, clear, bold shapes in a foreground against a more vague but intensely marked background may also give a sense of distance: for example, the observed leaves in the foreground set against the background foil of an indiscernible mass of leaf and flower shapes.

Line drawings are a good starting point for designing repeat motifs for embroidery, printing, patchwork, or even knitting. Linear drawings can be simplified and various repeat motif techniques tried – half drop, full

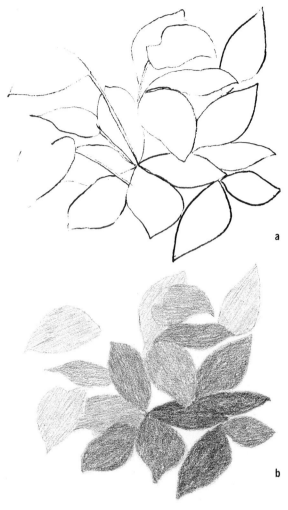

A line drawing using the same thickness of pen throughout. The build-up of marks is interesting, but the image has no depth. The large bold shapes at the top of the drawing representing rhododendrons bring the background forward. The detailed foreground helps to indicate that this is closer, but the concentration of marks may indicate otherwise – although the more careful foreground marks against the more haphazard background help somewhat. The problems created in this drawing might have been overcome if different thicknesses of pen had been used – thicker in the foreground, thinner towards the back – or, if worked in pencil, stronger marks could have been used in the foreground and softer marks in the distance

Patterns begin to emerge from the leaf shapes and their negatives

Exercises with leaves and tonal values **a** Line drawing where each line is drawn tonally to indicate the amount of light or shade on the edge of each leaf **b** Each leaf is represented by a tone which expresses the 'average' of the tonal values to be found on it **c** Each leaf is expressed by a number of different tones so that the angles of the leaves become apparent as they catch the light or are seen in shade

LEFT: Line drawing of leaf shapes. CENTRE: Drawing of leaf shapes on shaded ground to show positive and negative shapes. RIGHT: Leaf shapes shaded on a white ground. Negatives become clearer when linear qualities are removed from the drawing

Once shapes are defined and patterns emerge, simple motifs are easy to find and repeats can be tested for effect quite quickly

This drawing was made using three thicknesses of pen and a variety of qualities of mark. In the foreground the thick pen makes firm decisive lines and cross-hatching. The middle distance of lady's mantle becomes gradually less and less surely drawn as it recedes from the viewer. The background uses the finest pen and the marks become very sketchy, only hinting at garden subjects, stem and leaf shapes (by the author)

These two atmospheric drawings were worked in pencil with some areas erased and reworked. The final result is one of strength and confidence (Wendy Ward)

drop, mirror and so on. Try running these off on tracing paper, or make a number of photocopies to move around and play with.

Linear drawings can also be translated into mono-chromatic embroidery techniques – try drawing with a sewing machine, or simple straight stitch by hand. Quilting can also be an effective use of such drawings.

Linear drawings do not always adequately describe a subject, as can be seen from the leaf exercise. The shape of a pot may be enough to describe it as a pot, but much more will be known if the angle that the light was coming from is also described. It will then be clear whether any decoration was drawn or in relief. Leaf shapes, attractive in themselves, will begin to fall over one another and intertwine with the addition of light and shade.

Experiments with pencils will help in discovering which are most suitable for the effects desired and on which sort of paper. Small or large leaf shapes are a good place to start, or the closeknit texture of topiaried hedges will offer a quality of mark that can be used to describe the shapes and forms in the quantity of light and shade on the surface. These textures, drawn with a

The Lodge was worked in straight hand stitches from a pencil drawing. The embroidery as a whole represents the feeling of a visit which included the lodge. The area to the right of centre is a piece of dyed handmade paper which represents the view through the leaded-light windows on the lodge. The foreground embroidery of hand stitchery and loosely applied fabrics depicts the azaleas seen in the garden (Eva Kuniczak-Coles)

pencil or pen, whether smooth or scribbled, can be layered in increasing weights to describe the shadows, and placed on softly or barely at all where the subject is in full sunlight.

When drawing tonally, remember to use the extremes of tonal values available – from the pure white of the paper to the darkest marks that can be made with the medium. If necessary, record the range of tones being used in a 'shade card' at the side of the drawing so that this can be used for comparisons (this exercise may be difficult, as an infinite number of shades may be obtained with some media). The 'shade card' will make sure that full use is being made of the medium and, as comparisons are made, the drawing should stay lively throughout instead of gradually slipping into using fewer and fewer tones. This 'shade card' idea can also be useful for colour drawing and worksheets, and the 'shade card' can be taken on shopping trips to purchase fabrics or threads.

As well as working with pencil and charcoal and the smooth transitions that can be achieved with these media, try crosshatching with pencils, or using fibre-tip pens, or pen and wash, where progressively darker or more saturated washes can be added to the pen drawing. There are also fibre-tip pens available which 'bleed' when water is added, and these can make pen and wash much easier, although variety of tone is more difficult to achieve.

Try working up a whole picture in a range of tonal values with no line work at all – just select a shade for each area of the picture and blend it with the next, or leave strong contrasts as necessary. This exercise is particularly useful if a beginner has a tendency to draw strong lines around everything and 'colour in' the result. Remember that objects in nature do not have strong lines defining them, but are in fact defined by changes in light and shade and colour.

In drawings of gardens the light source will almost

Photograph of the knot garden at Barnsley House, Gloucestershire, showing the variety of textures available in hedging and evergreen trees. These marks and textures can be studied and used for the drawing of such subjects, making work with light and shade fairly easy as marks are laid on with increasing density in areas of heavy shadow

certainly be from above, and the greatest shade will be underneath the plants. This will help to define the positive shapes of the leaves themselves. Remember the lessons from the first drawings: negative shapes and apparently unworked areas are just as important as those of intense activity. This lesson will also be useful for embroidery, which needs quiet spaces as well as busy areas.

Different qualities can be created, textures taken away or toned down or blank areas added, by using an eraser to make inroads into or to lighten areas of pencil marks. These marks have an individual quality which could be sampled in textile techniques – try resist dyeing, or laying down organdie on areas of stitching,

This pen and wash sketch made use of the different qualities of mark available with a fine nib. The scratchy marks were particularly enjoyed and exploited (by the author)

This embroidery was worked quickly like the original sketch on silk, with nets, organdie and 'twinkle' fabrics added. The stitching is worked freely in black using a sewing machine, to keep the speed and freshness of touch (by the author)

or stitching but leaving blank areas like a free pattern-darning method. The best type of eraser to use is a kneadable one (putty rubber), available from all good artists' suppliers. This type of eraser can be pulled into small sections for careful work, will erase as much or as little as required according to the pressure exerted, and will not ruin the surface of the paper. It will also clean any unwanted marks off the surface when the drawing is finished.

Texture is perhaps more important in embroidery than in any other art form, and as such demands particular attention. When drawing in monochrome, pay attention to the textural aspects of the subject matter. For quilting, or work where the pattern of shapes is paramount, the textural qualities may seem less important, but even if the embroidery is based on shape, the textures of these shapes may become important. Practice with the media and the translation into stitch marks will help enormously. Do allow marks to influence one another – many stitch-type marks

work well in drawings. Allowing marks to cross over from one medium to another will stimulate new discoveries in all the media employed and lead to exciting and original work.

Tonal drawings can offer a starting point for a wide range of embroidery techniques. Layering of white and black organza, layering of hand and/or machine stitches, blackwork, pulled work, monotonal or monochromatic canvas work may all be suitable for indicating the textures and tones represented in the drawings. Even whitework or goldwork may seem suitable – see Chapter 7! Free stitching and collageing of fabrics on a fine or a coarse scale may also be appropriate, particularly if the drawing includes broad sweeps of shading mixed with areas of high textural interest.

Look at your drawings and try to decide what textile marks they most look like: this can form the starting point for the sampling which may then lead to creating a piece of work.

4

WORKING WITH COLOUR

'The elements of colour theory have been neither analyzed nor taught in our schools of art, because in France it is considered superfluous to study the laws of colour, according to the saying "Draughtsmen are made, but colourists are born." Secrets of colour theory? Why call these principles secrets which all artists must know and all should have been taught.'

Delacroix, Les Artistes de mon Temps

DRAWING and observation skills can be improved considerably by working in monochrome, but colour is vitally important both to gardens and to much embroidery. If the work is to progress, this will be done best by learning to make marks in colour. Colour mixing will improve as the media become more familiar, and learning to 'mash' the colours together for an all-over image will inspire embroidery.

Having attained a certain standard in monochromatic work, it is tempting to use this as a method of drawing and simply add notes or photographs for colour information. This may be adequate for some images – particularly those with very graphic qualities; but if the drawing is to capture the play of light on complicated shapes and mixtures of colour, this will best be achieved by drawing, painting or mark-making in colour.

Practise the exercises and techniques in Chapter 1 to become familiar with the materials. The easiest media to come to terms with are probably pencil crayons, oil pastels and gouache paints. Although soft pastels and acrylic paints offer interesting qualities of surface to the embroiderer, these are media best approached after a little experience has been gained.

Many people choose to start work with pencil crayons, regarding them as familiar materials from childhood! This can be dangerous, as notions taught to children of how crayons are to be used vary considerably from what will be best for embroidery, so try the experiments in Chapter 1 to loosen up before drawing. Learn to make colours and marks by experimenting on a separate sheet of paper, or make a colour and mark reference chart at the side of the drawing.

Learning to mix colours by layering will help to inspire colour mixing in embroidery, which can be achieved in much the same way. If a desired colour cannot be found, layers of different threads in hand or machine stitchery will create a colour from a distance, and close-up the effect will also be stunning as the purity of the individual threads becomes clear and they affect one another through contrast and harmony.

When mixing colours, avoid the use of black, unless it is actually present, as it will tend to muddy the image. Shade with complementary colours, or use colours from the cool part of the colour circle.

Watercolour pencil crayons mix well by layering and adding water, and further layers can be added and washed in much the same way as watercolour. Nevertheless, it is still important to choose as large a range as possible. Crayons, particularly the watercolour variety, will also be especially useful for worksheets, and the fact that paint, palettes, water and brushes are unnecessary, and that crayons do not need fixing, as well as being easy and clean to use, will make carrying them around and using them a much simpler option.

For the initial colour drawings, find an area that is not too complicated. At this stage avoid features that require perspective, such as pots, watering cans, long vistas with paths or topiary or steps. Choose instead an area of a flower border. If a tall herbaceous border is chosen, there will be many colours and textures to negotiate as well as a need to create an illusion of depth, light and shade.

When looking at the border it is tempting to try to include too much of it, so look through a viewfinder and try to compose the drawing. Do not start by making pencil marks: work straight away with the chosen medium. As the views chosen become more complicated, and perhaps include perspective, it may be necessary to make a few pencil marks as guidelines, but these should be kept to a minimum. Having decided how the view is going to fit on the paper, start with an area that offers a notion of how it can be tackled and work out from there. When painting it is often a good idea to put colour washes into areas first, and it is usually helpful to start at the back and work forwards, but it will be easier to start and achieve something encouraging if a drawing is begun where marks and colours are inspiring enough to answer any questions and difficulties about how they should be translated on to the paper.

Large areas of shading; small careful marks; layering of colour to add light, shade or different hues to a base colour, and changes in strengths of marks: all will add interest to the work whether in pastel, crayon or paint, and because the paperwork is more interesting it will be more inspiring when looking for embroidery ideas. 'Mash' the colours together until there are no white gaps. If separate flowers and leaves are drawn, there may be areas of blank paper left in between. This is not what you see in a herbaceous border – every area will be either some plant form, or possibly earth. In addition, these blank spaces will offer no source material for the embroidery – will the fabric be left blank in these areas? Every area of the paper must take on a colour or mixture of colour, a shade (a darker tone of a colour) or a tint (a lighter tone). If the blank paper seems intimidating or hard to 'fill', choose a creamy white or other pastel colour on which to start the drawing – but choose it carefully and appropriately

for the subject matter. Alternatively, start by painting, or laying down with pastel or crayon, a light colour wash over the whole surface of the paper. With experience, this colour wash could vary from area to area and so the drawing will begin. The fact that the paper is no longer stark white, whichever method is chosen, will help immensely in encouraging the first marks to be made, and in helping the whole drawing to come together as it develops.

There is rarely a time when a drawing is completed from start to finish and feels right all the way through. If a drawing seems to be going badly, do not despair. Nothing is ever learned by tearing up a drawing and starting again. Keep working on one drawing and things may start to 'gel'; first drawings always take a long time, so don't expect miracles in half an hour! If the results required cannot be achieved in the medium employed, then try mixing media to obtain a different or better result. Changing media can sometimes overcome a block. Certain marks will not always be easy in a new medium, so employ one that has already been mastered. Interesting results that emerge from mixed media can be very useful for inspiring embroidery. If the difficulty is with paint, and 'sampling' colours, textures and marks on a separate sheet or notebook is not helping, try adding pencil crayon or soft or oil pastel. The dexterity of mark available with these will certainly help if difficulties are being experienced with the control of the paint and brush. Adding such materials will create different effects on dry or wet paint. If the problem is making a soft pastel drawing 'gel', the addition of a paint wash may supply the required finish. Again, this wash could vary in colour or intensity to aid the drawing further.

If working in mixed media is inappropriate (perhaps a new medium is to be mastered at all costs!), try putting the unsuccessful drawing to one side and start working from the same subject matter in a different medium. This will give clues as to how to approach the mark-making in the first drawing. After a while, the first drawing can be resumed with increased confidence. The second drawing could also be completed, as a variety of drawings in different media can be very informative when the time comes to design the embroidery. The media for this second drawing should be chosen with care. Changing from oil pastels to crayons may help to uncover the marks that are being missed, as areas of intense colour which create an interesting and colourful blur, but no definition, are laid down. Using any crayon or pastel medium may offer textural possibilities that are being missed in paint. Each medium will have a way of informing the use of another, which should help, either through 'sampling' or working up another drawing when difficulties are

This painting was done quickly as the sky grew blacker before a rainstorm. Nevertheless it was fairly enjoyable as the usually crowded garden of Hidcote became increasingly deserted. First acrylic paint was applied, then more acrylic paint and oil pastels were added on to this drying surface – the final result was sketchy and messy, although the colours were pleasing. (Embroidery on p. 58)

encountered during a drawing or painting.

The idea of a sampler notepad has already been explored. Apart from holding the collection of exercises to help inspire marks whilst drawing in the garden, a notebook will also be useful for 'sampling' marks, colours, textures or brush strokes when needed for an actual drawing or painting. This sampling is similar to stitch sampling for embroidery and therefore a natural extension of the investigative process. Different textures can be tried by scribbling in different ways until the most suitable is found; brushstrokes can be tried out to gain confidence before a mark is made on the painting; colours can be mixed, remixed and compared, and notes can be made on how colours were obtained so that this information will be of use in the future; and objects can be drawn and redrawn until shapes and angles are better understood – particularly useful if perspective is still a problem. This sampler notepad can be kept and taken on field trips to help solve future problems. Additionally because the investigating is happening separately from the drawing, there will be less fear of trying new ideas, which means the drawing is likely to become more interesting and inventive. The marks discovered can be added to the drawing, and the 'sampler' notebook may also prove useful for helping with worksheet or embroidery samples, giving ideas on how it might be possible to proceed with the embroidery.

The size of the drawing paper is important. An adequately sized sheet is essential, especially for pastels and paint. The drawing may be finished to a smaller size, but if a sheet smaller than A2 is used the edge of the paper will make the marks on the drawing self-conscious and confined. An A3 sheet of paper may be fine for crayon drawings, which are naturally composed of smaller marks. But there is a tendency when using small sheets of paper to draw with the fingers and the wrist and make 'writing' marks. The drawing will also become over-concerned with small areas and detail. With a larger piece of paper it is possible to stand back and gain more of an overview of the drawing; details may only gradually become important. The mark-making is more likely to come from the elbow or shoulder and this will create a wider variety and choice in mark and scale. Starting out on a large sheet will not mean that all drawing will be finished to A1 size, but a new freedom will be found; as confidence in mark is achieved, and personal aims of drawing are gradually understood, it may be possible to adjust the size of paper used.

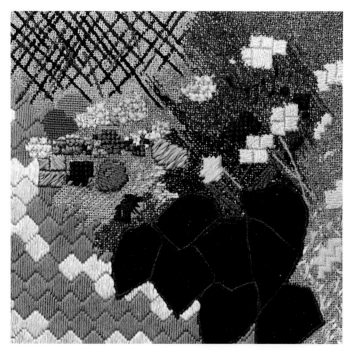

Cool garden: a place for thought. In this embroidery the crude marks become organised on the surface of the fabric. Worked by machine and hand, with ribbons and appliqué on to an 18 thread to 2.5 cm lockweave canvas. Lockweave is essential to prevent the threads pulling with machine stitching (by the author)

Colours and marks can be placed down in broad sweeps of movement, but the careful addition of light and shade will help to make the final image more real and rounded as well as giving a greater sense of distance. Choose colours from the cooler side of the colour circle – blue/green is the coolest colour, but the apparent darkness that indigo, purple or violet offer can be more successful. These can be used to add shadow and depth to an image. Use them in a wash of crayoning or paint underneath or over the top of existing colour. Worked carefully, these 'washes' can add shadow to a leaf or flower, or shade underneath areas that are in light. Violet, deep blue or blue/grey added to an area in a light 'wash' or all-over light crayoning will give the impression of things receding into the distance. This is because, as things become distant, there is more air between the viewer and the object viewed. The feeling of this distant separation by cool air can be captured by the addition of cool colours. Distance can also be indicated by sketchier drawing or adding blue/grey to the colours so that they lose their distinctive qualities.

Lighter, warmer colours will give the impression of sunlight shining on a subject. The warmest colour is red/orange, so choose warm colours from those grouped around this side of the colour circle. Yellow has a brightness to the eye, a particular characteristic

of this colour, and can thus be used to indicate areas that are flooded with light.

A drawing worked solely on the principle of warm and cool colours can be highly successful, as the Impressionists discovered. Look, for example, at the work of Cézanne and Monet. Monet made particular use of harmonious and clashing colour schemes, so his work can be highly informative in its colour use. Colour mixing was also a preoccupation of the Neo-Impressionists – the pointilism of Seurat and Signac shows a simpler way of putting down and mixing colours (try using fibre-tip pens) which also provides a source of inspiration for embroidery design.

Complementary colours can also be used to add shading to an object, as will have been seen from the experiments in Chapter 1. If using cooler colours to shade seems inappropriate, perhaps because the object is too near, try using complementaries. Shading expressed in this way can be effective, and the difficult colour that was so hard to comprehend in the shadowed area of a daffodil will be easily rendered by adding violet. This technique can be used subtly, as in the work of Degas, or more boldly, as in that of the Post-Impressionists, such as Van Gogh.

Colours can be chosen to create harmonious effects (if they are chosen from related areas on the colour circle), or they may clash (if they are totally unrelated). Collections of complementary colours can be painted to create an exciting effect that is nevertheless satisfying to the eye.

The mood that is desired in a drawing can be heightened by using the effects offered by colour – cool or warm, harmonising or contrasting. These will help in the expression of a general feeling. The subject matter itself may help to decide this: a water garden will almost certainly provide for a harmonious drawing; the Red Garden at Hidcote in Gloucestershire, or the courtyard worked completely in purples and yellows with red paving, terracotta pots and red yuccas against a deep green hedge, would provide an excellent subject for exercises with complementary colours. But complementaries can also be found in more subtle gardens and highlighted in the nature of the drawing.

A conservatory garden provides an excellent subject where control over what is emphasised can be exercised (conservatories have the added advantage of providing a garden subject in mid-winter). Should the drawing concentrate on the qualities of shades of green from the lime shades through to the deep blue/greens? Complementary reds (against all the greens) may be available in the colours of the floor, the stems of palms or the red underside of some leaves; or can complementary colours be used for the shading? Or should the drawing be concerned with the warmth of

This drawing and photograph of the same subject show the 'licences' that can be taken with a subject. The statue, only just visible on the photograph, was enlarged as a point of interest for the drawing. This combination of images is successful in the drawing, and if the view was seen in life then the attention of the eye would be taken by the unusual statue in the distance through the gap in the hedge. The colours and marks in the drawing fade and become greyer as they become more distant (by the author)

the conservatory – the warm of the solid surfaces reflecting the heat, the pool surround, the flooring, any metalwork, contrasting with the coolness of the greens in the leaves, or the splashing of a fountain and the depths of a pool.

The choice of harmony, clash, contrast or cool/warm should not be arbitrary. Allow the subject matter to indicate which method of approach will be most suitable; perhaps different areas of the drawing may require different treatments.

The drawing position for colour work should ideally be one where the board is upright. Take a few steps back from the work from time to time to see how it is progressing, and whether areas that are receiving individual attention are beginning to work together as a whole. I like to take colours and use them across the whole drawing (not my own invention, but one used by many painters). A little of a colour may be added here, some more of it there: it may be used for shading across a larger area somewhere else, or used to

underlie another colour elsewhere. Although in some areas this colour may only underlie or overlie a more predominant colour, the fact that the colours are 'travelling' across the surface of the work, and not being isolated to this flower here and that flower there, will make the whole drawing more successful. Again, this notion of 'travelling' colour will be effective in embroidery. Standing back from a piece of work will reveal where this movement of colour can be successfully employed. The drawing can be seen as a whole and marks and washes laid down that will bring the piece together.

Often the first drawings can look a little like samplers. Each flower maintains a remoteness from its neighbour, each colour is placed in just the right area, this flower is blue, this one yellow, and so on. Only through observing the background and tangle of leaves, and making colours 'travel' across the surface, will this situation be improved. Look carefully at the way each plant interferes with its neighbour. In an

This drawing in soft pastels was done by a newcomer to the medium, but nevertheless captures the quality of the water (Judy Cummins)

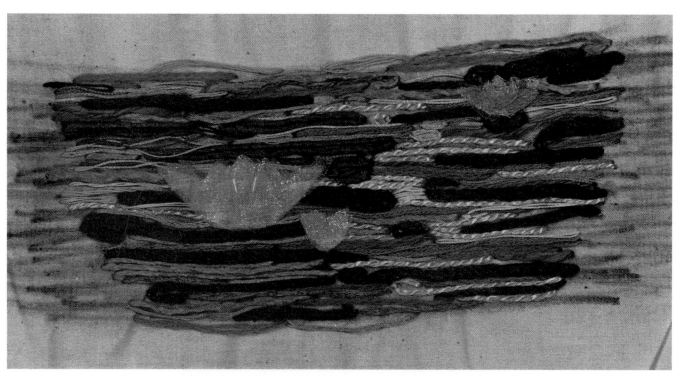

Embroidery sample worked from drawing above on dyed calico with a variety of threads and dyed organdie. The main stitch is a long-armed chain stitch (Judy Cummins)

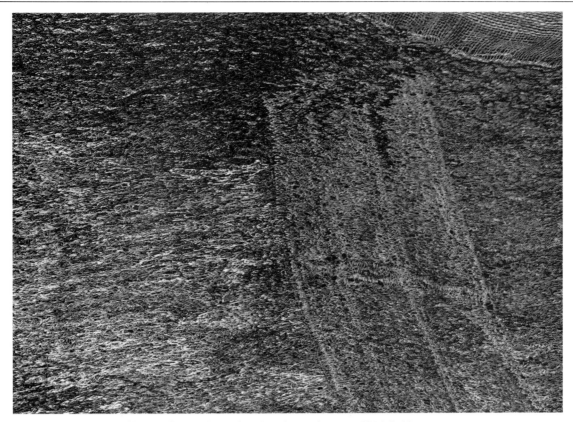

Close-up of embroidery in the colour photograph on page 75. Worked by machine on coloured scrim from a drawing done in Monet's garden. The work is done entirely with a zigzag stitch to build up a coloured, textured surface on the fabric. The reflection included is of Monet's famous Japanese bridge

herbaceous bed it is not easy to define the edge of one plant and the beginning of another; if the drawing recognises the overlap and intertwining of plants, it will look less like a sampler! If the first drawings look like 'samplers' they may offer ideas for repeat motifs or blackwork (which could be worked in colour).

Drawing water is something that many people find difficult. There are, however, several methods which will prove effective in capturing its qualities. First, consider that there are many colours in water. It will be reflecting all the colours within the surrounding area, either recognisably or as just dashes of this shade and that. Secondly, water is always cooler than the surrounding environment, so choose colours from the cooler side of the circle for its main body. Thirdly, water will almost certainly be on the move, if only slightly, so it will move in horizontal ripples – therefore use horizontal strokes to describe it. Even if the water is very still, start with horizontal movements of colour and gradually blend them to merge into a surface. Any splashes of fountains or falls can be added to the basic drawing; white water, splashing and tumbling, can be explained by using resist techniques, such as oil pastels under water-based paint or a watercolour-resist medium. These techniques can be used for both paperwork and embroidery. Water is a feature of many gardens: it adds coolness to a hot courtyard, or space and tranquillity to a northern garden. A good drawing will aid the eventual working of an embroidery which embodies these qualities, and as water is used in so many gardens, the fear of dealing with it, on paper or in embroidery, is worth overcoming.

Drawing and painting cause much nervousness and people are often loath to start for fear of making a fool of themselves. The execution of a good drawing can look fairly easy when done by someone with a little experience; they seem to achieve the desired effect with little or no effort, and so quickly. This confidence will only come with perseverance. Even the most competent artist has probably spent time in front of a blank piece of paper wondering how to start or, later, how to finish! But even when the drawing looks effortless, it is not. Any artist will be tired after a day spent drawing or painting, as concentration on the subject and on the capabilities of the media have to be consistent if the result is to be worthwhile.

Oil pastel of Birmingham Botanical Gardens. Note the warm terracottas against the cool blue/green leaves (by the author)

Conservatory worked from the oil pastel on the left. The silk ground is dyed with silk dye. Hand stitches, layers of see-through fabrics and additional dyeing with fibre-tip dyes was then added (by the author)

RIGHT: Machine embroidery in scrim worked from the pencil crayon drawing in the conservatory at Birmingham Botanical Gardens on page 71 (by the author)

This photograph was taken of part of the Lutyens house in Le Parc des Moutiers at Verangeville-sur-Mer in France, as a record of the image. But the image itself changed through the drawing process and embroidery in order to create a flat surface and create more plant growth, whilst retaining both windows

It is always tempting, as the drawing seems to take longer than anticipated, to take a photograph. The argument will be that the camera can record any additional information, so that the drawing can be finished off at home. Both of these statements are unlikely to be true, and the photograph will once again be relied on for the embroidery. The information gathered will be poorer because the 'prop' of the camera rendered real observation unnecessary. As I have outlined, cameras should only be used for information that you are not capable of recording yourself – at this stage the only problems may be with perspective, which the flat quality of the photographic image will certainly help with. Time should not be a consideration. An embroidery is likely to take some time to create, and any time spent drawing will be valuable, as it increases an understanding of the subject and helps in discerning exactly the elements that are important for the ensuing work. Choose a garden where time will not be a problem – a large

amount of good information is invaluable when working out the embroidery on worksheets and in samples.

Once the drawing is completed, a photograph may be taken for documentary reasons – what the camera saw and what was individually recorded on the drawing may be very different, although this will not necessarily mean that the drawing is bad. It is important that everyone has their own view of the world. Moods that a camera will not be able to capture can be created by an individual: this is what makes the drawing process so important, and what will make an embroidery thus designed unique.

Using photographs for embroidery does have a tendency to cause the result to be fairly photographic in its response. Creating realism in textiles is not difficult and, unless a great deal of time is spent at the worksheet stage developing the images gained from photography, realism is the natural response. Making worksheets from photographs can also be difficult, as

Watercolour sketches of Le Parc des Moutiers. I included many of the features that seemed important – the capping on the walls, the brick pillars, the house with climbing plants, windows and details. Its lack of success as a composition led me to try cutting it in three to achieve more interesting compositions and groups. Thus I noticed, and became interested in, the windows of the house

This watercolour sketch was worked from the view of the building incorporated in the photograph

certain areas of information may be missing unless a good collection of photographs from one image or similar images is available. If new boundaries are to be discovered for the individual, for the craft and in imagery, this is more likely if the work is taken from completely original material.

A good colour drawing will often be directly translatable into embroidery. Hand and machine stitchery can recreate many marks; layered fabrics or dyes can represent the overlaying qualities of thinned paint; textural surfaces made with oil pastel or acrylic can be achieved with collaging of fabrics or a heavy use of hand or machine stitches.

If a drawing does not immediately suggest something – perhaps the composition is unsatisfactory or incomplete, or perhaps the wish is to develop the work into something more than a direct visual translation of an image – no matter how different the image is from the original garden it will still be possible to push it further. Perhaps something is to be made for an interior or for wearing? Or perhaps an embroidery can be created that is further abstracted until it only reminds one of the original garden and is now simply an embroidery, rather than an embroidered garden.

In order to push the existing images in these different directions, start experimenting on worksheets and sampling ideas in embroidery and textiles. These processes are an excellent path to discovery and invention, and will be discussed further in Chapter 6.

5

ADDING ANOTHER
DIMENSION

*'Perspective is an invention of architects ... but I
am thrilled by the way Chinese scrolls manifest a different attitude
towards space.'*

David Hockney, 1988

DEPTH of field can be indicated by the coarseness or
heaviness of line giving way to pale and uncertain
qualities, or to heavier but indistinct shading. Colour
changes can also be used to indicate it. Forms can be
described by the careful use of shading which indicates
the source of light, and thus the three-dimensional
form of an object. But, sooner or later, images and
subject matter that cannot be portrayed by these
methods alone may be required. This is where the
knowledge of perspective can prove useful.

Perspective often seems daunting to the
inexperienced artist, but it need not be. There are basic
rules which are easily mastered. Once these rules are
understood they can be followed slavishly – the
perspective of each element of every drawing carefully
worked out – or used simply to inform the drawing
process. Perspective does not always need to be worked
out exactly, as long as there is an awareness of which
lines ought to be vanishing where, or roughly how
circles and ellipses (circles in perspective) should be
seen in relation to each other. A notebook can always
be used whenever an object is posing a particular
difficulty: it can be worked out carefully, using the
rules learned. Once the object or problem is understood,
it can be drawn on to the main piece of work.

Learning to use perspective will also add an assured

third dimension to embroidery – one that is often
avoided. Once perspective has been understood, a
subject that avoids it can be chosen, if preferred.
Indeed, the full knowledge of perspective may only
rarely be used but, even if the drawing is only of a pot
with some flowers, the following will prove invaluable
and the subject surprisingly easy.

Perspective is often not required, even in difficult
drawings, as comparative distances and angles can be
checked without the use of any technical formula, as
long as care is taken. How tall one object is in relation
to another; at what angle a branch leaves the trunk of
a tree; the pitch of an archway; the distance between
objects – all of these things can be determined by using
a pencil as a measuring tool. There is a cliché of the
artist holding a pencil up in front of one eye and
moving it around, but, done properly, this can answer
many of the construction problems in a drawing.

Hold the pencil at arm's length – do not have a bent
elbow (it will be impossible to know how bent it was
next time a comparative measurement is made) – and
line the end of the pencil up with the top of the object
that is being measured. Place a thumb at the position
on the pencil where the bottom of the object is seen.
This method can be used for comparing verticals,
horizontals and relative distances throughout a

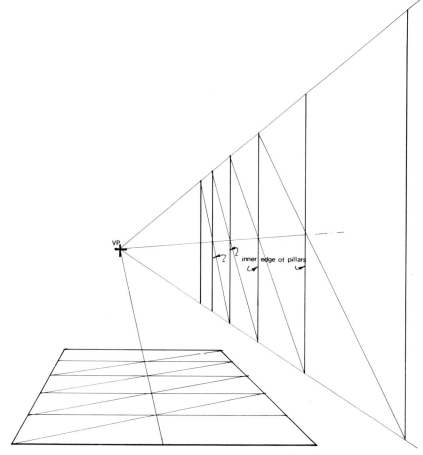

In order to draw posts moving further away (and as they do so, moving closer together), bisect the post equally, then draw a line from this point to the vanishing point. Draw two pillars. The next pillar will be drawn on a vertical where a diagonal drawn across the centre of the second pillar from the base of the first, intersects the line representing the top of all the pillars. Having drawn the third pillar, the fourth can be worked out similarly. This method also works for paving, railings, equidistant trees, etc.

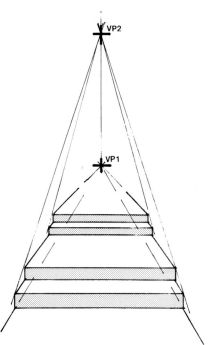

Working out steps seen straight on. The first vanishing point is the same as those used for the other parts of the drawing. The second is directly above the first and indicates how the sides of the steps should be drawn. In the final drawing this information would not be necessary as plants cover the edges of the steps – a useful trick if perspective proves difficult in a drawing

drawing. When placing the relative distances on to the drawing, the exact lengths measured can be reproduced (only mark one distance at a time). If this is not satisfactory, (the drawing will usually be larger in scale) then simply multiply the measured lengths appropriately to suit the drawing. This method of being able to relate measurements is essential for more complicated drawings of gardens with many and various forms.

To compare angles, simply hold the pencil at arm's length so that it runs the length of the diagonal being studied. The angle of the pencil will appear clear and will be easy to compare with the verticals and horizontals that already exist on the paper, allowing the problem angle to be drawn by making these comparisons.

Perspective can be enjoyed and employed as a useful science of space; it can also be ignored or deliberately

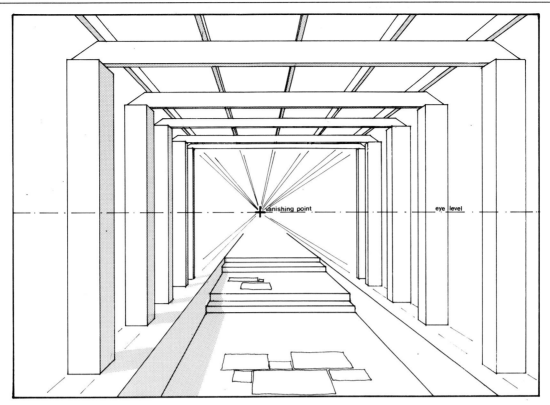

This line drawing, taken directly from the photograph on page 72, illustrates
how one-point perspective is constructed

overturned – consider the work of Matisse, Picasso or Braque, for example. Whether it is to be used or wilfully ignored, an understanding of the science itself is important. Any attempts to deal with space must be accurate if the illusion is to be complete. Alternatively, perspective laws and convention on spatial relationships can be contravened if there is an awareness of normal conventions. If perspective is understood, informed choices about the treatment of space can be made.

Perspective can be applied to any object, from a pathway, road, or house with windows, to pots, walls, steps, people and even leaf and flower shapes.

The illustrations show where the knowledge of perspective will be useful and how to use it. Once an area where perspective is needed can be recognised, it is not difficult to employ. Alternatively, by learning where perspective is avoidable, a subject where it can be avoided can be chosen. Either of these courses of action is preferable to the results if subjects which do require perspective are drawn and ignorance becomes apparent in the uneasiness of the handling of the finished drawing.

Our knowledge of the surrounding world – that two opposite sides of a box are equal, that the sides of a path do not converge – makes the drawing of certain objects difficult. What is known to be true conflicts with what is seen and what will have to be drawn if the illusion of three dimensions on a flat piece of paper is to be satisfactory.

The use of perspective will overcome these problems. The most basic illustration is in one-point perspective. First, the height of the horizon must be decided. The horizon may not actually be visible: it may be obscured by hedges, trees, flowers or a rising landscape. This does not have to cause problems – the horizon is at your eye level and will change according to whether you are sitting or standing. It may be possible to discern an object that marks this level, or a line leading away towards the vanishing point may seem totally horizontal, and this will give the eye level.

Next, imagine that you are standing in the middle of a path that is disappearing towards the horizon. Lines representing the sides of the path will converge towards the vanishing point. If there are pillars at the side of the path, then a line drawn along the top of the pillars will meet the lines already drawn at the vanishing point on the horizon. If a pergola structure is spread between the pillars, it will have lines that meet at the same vanishing point, as will any lines representing the sides of paving stones leading away from you. All these lines will meet at one vanishing point which is on your eye level directly ahead of you. The pillars seem to get closer together as they get further away, and the

Watercolour and soft pastel drawing of the pool in Monet's garden at Giverny.
Space is flattened in the pool reflections (by the author)

LEFT: Drawing with pencil crayons in Birmingham Botanical Gardens. Again this drawing features the warm shades of the conservatory construction and pool, against the cooler shades of the leaves. The red and orange tones in some of the leaves increase the feeling of heat. The perspective of the pool shape, windows and wrought iron work is carefully worked out (by the author)

RIGHT: Conservatory at Birmingham Botanical Gardens, worked in machine embroidery on scrim from an oil pastel (by the author)

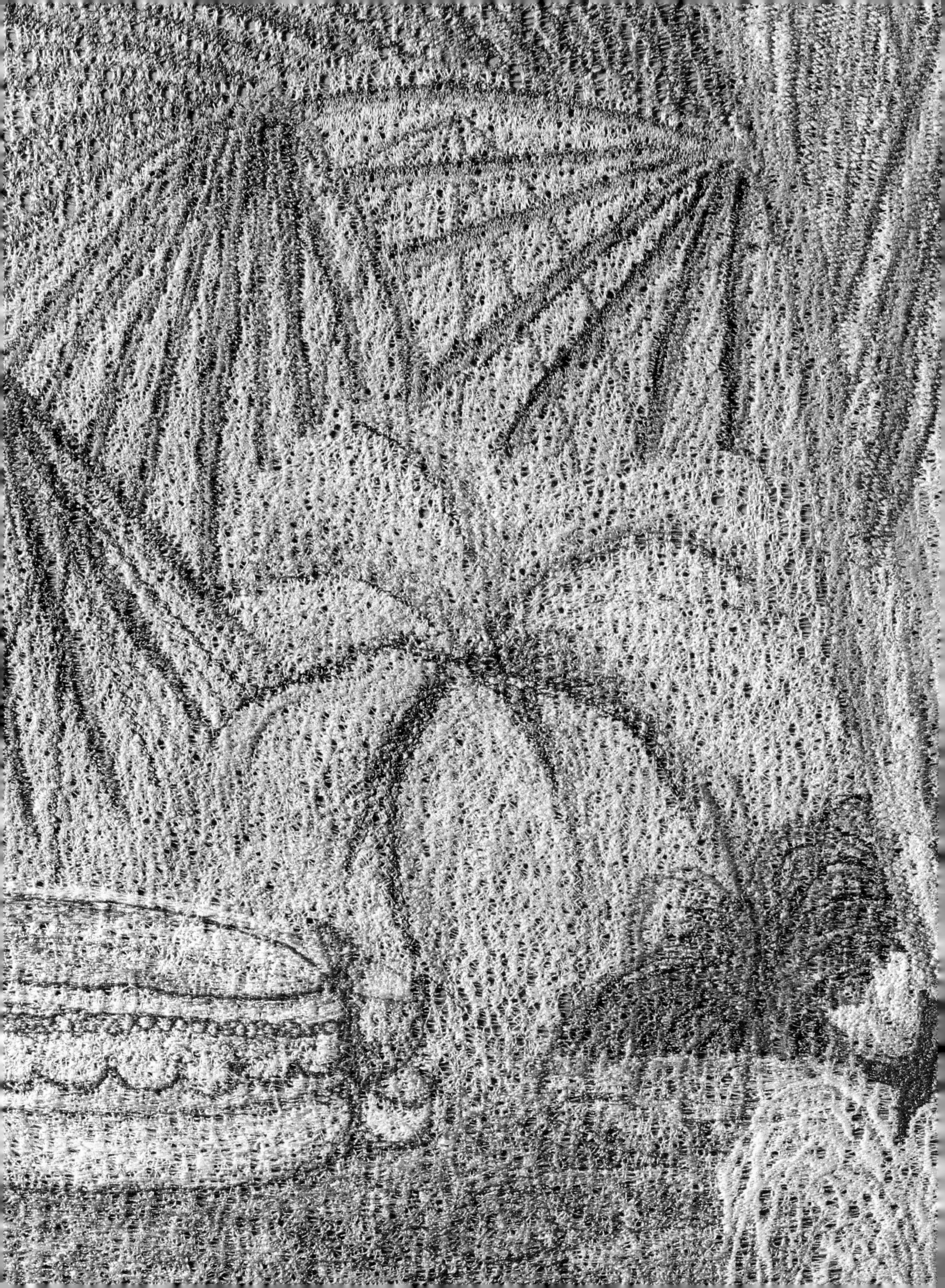

This photograph illustrates a view where one-point perspective should be used.
Le Parc des Moutiers, France (see pages 68 and 69)

paving stones become smaller. This can be worked out carefully, but once you are aware of the principles involved, it is possible to make a drawing without recourse to such detailed effort, although it is as well to practise with perspective, or make some preliminary notes about a view in a notebook or sketchbook first.

The change of levels in a series of steps can also be worked out using perspective. The lines visible at the side of the treads will all meet at the same vanishing point, which is at eye level. The sloping wall, banister, or points representing the front of each step will converge on a second vanishing point, which will be above eye level and can be decided on by holding up a pencil to discern the angle of one side of the steps. The second side can be constructed to match, bearing in mind that the second vanishing point is directly above the first.

Of course things are not always so simple, and a view or an object may diminish in two directions, neither of which is directly ahead. The principle here is the same as in one-point perspective, only there are now two points. For example, each side of the boxed hedge design, seen at an angle, will follow to a different

vanishing point. All parallel lines will correspond to one another and lead to the same vanishing point. Whereas in one-point perspective two parallel sides of a square shape were represented by horizontals, now all parallels lead to one vanishing point or the other. If a number of square or box shapes were strewn haphazardly across the picture each object would have its own two vanishing points at eye level, and it would only be coincidence if either of these vanishing points were shared with any other object.

Just to complicate matters, if steps are seen at an angle, two vanishing points are needed on the horizon, plus an additional vanishing point above the first one for the convergence of the sides of the steps.

Perspective is a fascinating subject, and if structure becomes important to the types of views that interest you, careful study can offer many benefits in creating the illusion of space. I have included a further reading list (page 141) should this prove necessary.

Perspective can also be useful for garden drawing where pots or other cylindrical objects are to be included. If the nature of an ellipse (a circle seen in perspective) can be recognised through practising ellipses and understanding how they are constructed, then the free drawing of round objects will improve when these are included. The drawing of cylinders is based on the drawing of boxes in perspective, with circles or ellipses added. Note that there is no sharp point where the ellipse joins the sides of the cylinder. For pot shapes, simply construct two ellipses and join them together. Any decoration on the pot will also follow an ellipse and will not simply be a straight line. Once ellipses are understood, practise drawing them freehand on a piece of paper; these can then be added to the final drawing. The construction of correct ellipses through the drawing of squares or cubes in perspective can be time-consuming, and is in fact unnecessary once there is an understanding of what is required. Again, notebook practice will help.

Perspective in the drawing of plants can also be useful, although it is usually unnecessary unless a very botanical result is required. Plants can be seen to be made up of shapes within squares or rectangles which require perspective, or stems and flowers which can be constructed out of cylinders and ellipses. This will normally only be useful if a foreground subject needs to be recorded with extreme accuracy – careful observation will suffice for most drawings. If a particular difficulty is experienced in understanding a plant form, or indeed any object, well enough to draw it, then it is useful to be able to use a notebook and investigate the perspective until it is understood well enough to make the drawing.

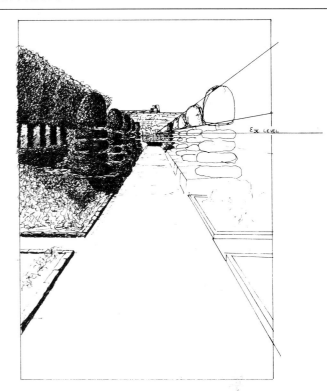

The herb garden in Villandry in the Loire Valley. One-point perspective is used to make sense of this view – I have left one side incomplete to show the construction. There is a strong light source, as the sun is fairly low towards the end of the day. This causes long shadows, which add form as well as an atmosphere to the drawing. The eye level seems high in relation to the buildings: this is because the garden is raised – the houses of the village over the wall are built on a road that is much lower than the path from which the view is taken

The knot gardens, fences and arbours in this photograph of Villandry would require two-point perspective; the steps would require the use of a third point

Watercolour, soft and oil pastel drawing of Monet's garden at Giverny. Again the pool is the subject of interest, but the fronds of a weeping willow and the reflection of the Japanese bridge are included. Space is flattened in the reflections, creating an 'abstract' appearance (by the author)

Embroidery worked by machine on coloured scrim with varying widths of zigzag mostly worked at right-angles to the machine. The scrim is held in a frame, but the stitching only catches and pulls around threads in a fairly unpredictable manner which is the charm of this technique (by the author)

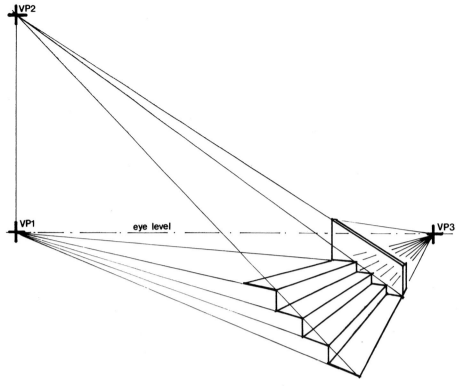

Diagram to show how steps seen at an angle are constructed using three-point perspective

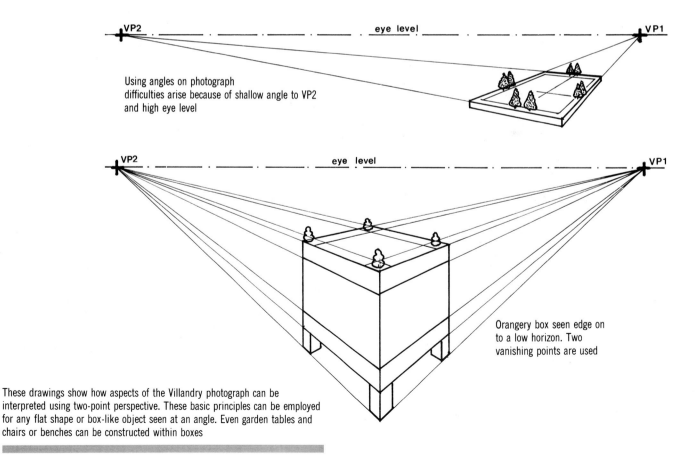

Using angles on photograph difficulties arise because of shallow angle to VP2 and high eye level

Orangery box seen edge on to a low horizon. Two vanishing points are used

These drawings show how aspects of the Villandry photograph can be interpreted using two-point perspective. These basic principles can be employed for any flat shape or box-like object seen at an angle. Even garden tables and chairs or benches can be constructed within boxes

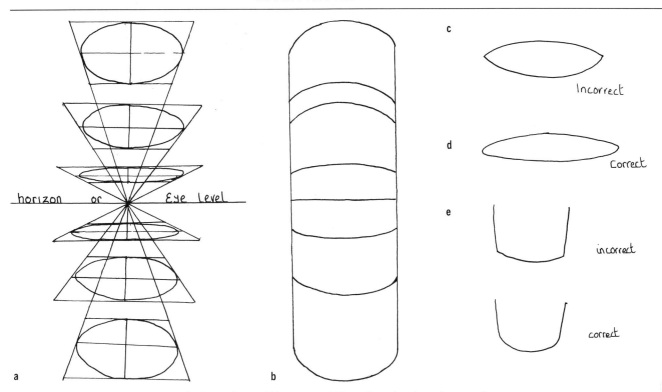

a

b

c   Incorrect

d   Correct

e   incorrect

correct

Circles are drawn within squares, which are themselves drawn in perspective
a a series of circles are shown as ellipses drawn in different relationships below
and above eye level b This information is translated into a drawing of a tubular
form. The lines on the tube indicate where any pattern would follow. Note that
at eye level a circle or ellipse is represented by a straight line c Ellipses do not
have points d Ellipses are drawn as a continuous curve e This continuous curve
moves gently into a vertical if there is one present – as on a pot

A round lead pot on rounded steps makes a good study for ellipses. The
structural and textural interest of this view, coupled with overgrowing plants,
would make an excellent subject for an embroidery

This photograph of the view on page 78 is evidence that reasonable accuracy
can be achieved without painstaking constructions, after a little experience has
been gained, and with very careful observation

Drawing three dimensions on to a flat surface need not be difficult. Various tricks can be used in monochrome and colour, and all is possible with the science of perspective. Any subject in the garden can be chosen without restriction. The choice may seem a little daunting, so pay particular attention to composition. Choose a subject where the qualities of tone and texture are evenly balanced, or deliberately chosen for their imbalance. Bear in mind whether the colour scheme is to harmonise or contrast. Consider how the image is to be composed. Is the eye to be led into the picture? How will interest be sustained? Will the image be framed in any way? Is there a focal point or a number of focal points?

As drawing skills develop and subject matter no longer needs to be restricted, careful choice of the subject matter or view must be made. Choose carefully and investigate thoroughly. Gather enough information to embark on worksheets, samples, and, finally, the

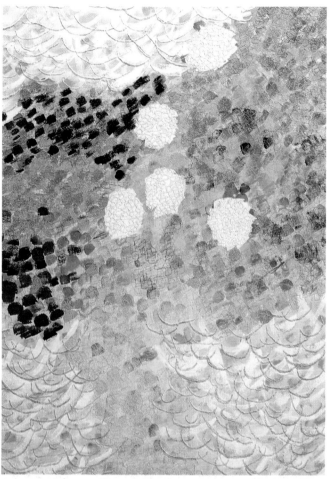

RIGHT: Worked from an acrylic painting made in Hidcote Gardens, Gloucestershire. The image is painted on a calico backing and embroidered by machine (Lisa Collier)

Working drawing for colour photograph on page 79. Acrylic paint applied to paper with a small palette knife, worked in Hidcote Gardens (Lisa Collier)

Drawing of a view at Barnsley House, Gloucestershire. This drawing was made without any lines for the perspective being worked out in advance, but the knowledge of perspective informed the lines and marks that were made (by the author)

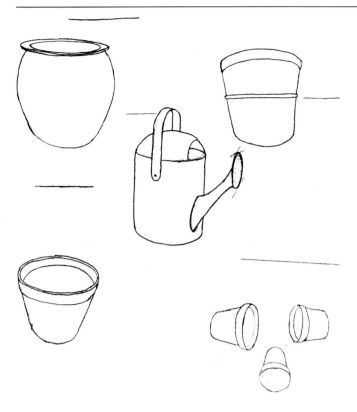

embroidery. The drawing skills learned and the understanding of the subject built up throughout the drawing process will assist the embroidery. By understanding the subject thoroughly, it will be possible to impart a chosen aspect to the viewer, whether this is how the view looked, how it felt, or how it excited interest. In order to impart a particular notion as successfully as possible, worksheets and samples must be made so that this notion can be distilled into a textile medium. The following chapter gives advice on finding exactly the image that is required from a series of drawings or photographs, and then sampling in textile media to find out how to portray such images.

Flower pots and a watering can drawn with different eye levels (represented by the line)

Leaves and flowers can be constructed within ellipses or squares and rectangles using the techniques already discussed. The distance in these two computer-generated images is created with size of shapes as well as perspective. Using the computer, different qualities of shading were also tried out. The images were worked as a design for a canvas work kit from the Red Garden at Hidcote Manor (Sarah Beecham)

6

WORKSHEETS AND SAMPLES

*'May I use a simile, the simile of the tree? The artist has studied
this world of variety and has, we may suppose, unobtrusively
found his way in it. His sense of direction has brought
order into the passing stream of image and experience. This sense
of direction in nature and life, this branching and spreading
array, I shall compare with the root of the tree. From the root the
sap flows to the artist, flows through him, flows to his eye.
Thus he stands as the trunk of the tree.
Battered and stirred by the strength of the flow, he moulds his vision
into his work.
As, in full view of the world, the crown of the tree unfolds
and spreads in time and in space, so with his work.'*

Paul Klee, *On Modern Art*, 1924 (translated by Paul Findlay)

RESPONSES to images are as varied as individuals, but it is often difficult to define exactly a personal response to something, even when the images to be portrayed seem very clearly defined in the mind. Through drawing and re-drawing something; through entering into a discussion about weights of tone, texture, colour and composition; through negotiating what the image is going to be – a hanging, picture, interior design object, or wearable: a dialogue in worksheets and samples will help clarify what this personal response is.

Often a response to an image is one that has been influenced too much by other embroideries which may have been worked from similar imagery. Worksheets and samples will help in the move away from an initial response.

Sometimes when looking at a collection of images that are found to be interesting, no immediate textile solution springs to mind. Again, worksheets and samples will help in the process of discovering how such images can become an embroidery.

There is often a danger, as an experienced or inexperienced embroiderer, that all responses to all imagery are the same, and that these are not progressing: in fact, that the work is in a rut. Using worksheets and pushing the ideas that come from these images into textile samples will lead to a new direction and line of thought. Work may be slow to change, but worksheets will help.

There are times when an image can be understood, and the embroidery and the response required can be worked out from the drawing process alone.

The work on *Le Parc des Moutiers* illustrates this. My first watercolour sketches (Chapter 4) indicated what interested me about the house and garden – that it is a fairly stern building with things growing up it and over it. I was also particularly inspired by the windows –

Two worksheets of inspiration for embroidery and embroideries and garden samples (Sonya Head)

Worksheet on a glasshouse theme from a garden in the Lake District. The design developed in a pictorial way using paint, fabrics and machine embroidery (Kay Bragg)

An embroidery worked for the project in Chapter 7. The ground is dyed silk noile with layered transparent fabrics for the water. Stitching is by hand in a variety of threads. The border is of pearl cottons wrapped over card, the embroidery is then framed with card covered with dyed silk (Sue Jones)

Embroidery from glasshouse worksheet. The ground is of layered fabrics with machine and hand stitching. The conservatory frame is of quilted silk noile over card. The inner conservatory ridge is trapunto quilting (Kay Bragg)

typical of a Lutyens house. The next watercolour defined a view that included these points of interest. I also wanted to indicate the heat of the day, and that I had enjoyed warm and sunny weather throughout my French trip. The gardens themselves were important, and I wished to show how colourful they were, not just in June, but throughout the year. I had also visited Giverny on the previous day, and, as Monet and other Impressionists had worked in and around Verangeville-sur-Mer, it seemed appropriate that this should also influence me. In the final oil pastel I aimed to say all these things. Having defined exactly how I wanted to say them, a direct translation into embroidery was all that was required. The technique of machine embroidery on scrim is one that I have developed and wished to develop further, and it also recreates the feeling of oil pastel rather well. The title *Le Parc des Moutiers – an Impression* bears witness to the piece being an impression of my being there, and how it looked to me under the circumstances described, but

also suggests Monet's *Sunrise – an Impression*, or *Impression of a Sunrise*, which gave the movement its name.

As an individual approach to embroidery is developed, it is possible to fall into a pattern of developing ideas through many drawings and working the embroidery in what becomes a personal style. But even for the experienced embroiderer a return to working out ideas thoroughly through worksheets and samples can have surprisingly refreshing results. For the novice, it is essential if the problems associated with discovering interesting and individual textile responses to images are to be overcome.

So what is a worksheet and how can it help? Ideas come in a progression of thoughts. If these are worked out in the head, difficulties that arise with technique, composition, or some other problem may be skipped over. If each idea is recorded, this will help to eliminate some problems and show up others. As each idea is recorded it will lead to new solutions and new ideas,

This pastel drawing of a garden was the starting point for a worksheet looking at leaf qualities in embroidery (Joan Broom)

This worksheet includes pencil and pastel drawings of leaves and embroidery samples. Starting at the top and working round to the left: two samples of machine stitched lace on vanishing fabric, dyed and quilted with a satin stitched edge, layered coloured see-through fabrics machine stitched, machine quilting on silk (Joan Broom)

and these, too, can be recorded. Recording these ideas in words is not adequate – after all, if a pictorial image could be described in words there would be very little point in making it. (Madame Rambert once said something similar when asked to describe a dance – if a dance could be put into words there would be no point in dancing it.) By recording all ideas in pictorial images, and sampling in appropriate media if this becomes the nature of the inquiry, it is possible to answer questions thoroughly, and to evolve new questions to be answered and new solutions and ideas. So, all ideas must be recorded in an appropriate visual format, either through drawing in various media or sampling with textiles and threads.

Ideas will progress much easier if all this work can be viewed fairly readily, and preferably at one time (a pin-board where all the work can be placed can be very useful). As a road to the realisation of an idea is followed, there will inevitably be ideas that do not follow the same route. These ideas can also be recorded as they may inform the final piece; or be the starting point of a new idea on another occasion; or, if one train of thought does not lead to fruition, they can be returned to and pursued. If all the ideas that occur on a particular theme are drawn on or attached to one sheet of paper, or a series of sheets, it will be easier to identify the route that is being taken to the realisation of an idea and thus pursue it. Any information from drawings and samples worked on earlier sheets will also be readily accessible, and this may still be helpful and informative as the design reaches fruition.

Worksheets help the individual to define a route, its problems and solutions, and help anyone else to see how a certain solution was arrived at (this may be important for examination or commission work).

Worksheets should examine an idea, ask questions about it, offer solutions (many more than one!), include samples of any techniques required and lead to a final discussion on how a piece may be made. They should be able to inform how this process has been executed and how the solution has been arrived at. They will tell a story about a process of investigation, and the progress of an idea, and can often do all this without a single word being written!

Worksheets can be used to investigate many different questions, and thus find a variety of solutions.

The Red Garden at Hidcote. Hand embroidery on a dyed evenweave ground.
The stitching is worked by hand and includes traditional blackwork techniques
as well as free stitching (Kate Wormington)

Sample worked from drawing of the Red Garden at Hidcote, using herringbone stitch and cross stitch (Kate Wormington)

RIGHT: Pot plant worked as a stumpwork sample. The flowers are free needlemade lace worked up from the ground fabric. The leaves are needlemade lace over padding (Eileen Bissell)

Drawings were made in water-soluble oil pastel and crayon of water gardens
with lilies and surrounding weeping trees. Machine embroidery was tried on
scrim and dyed fabrics using machine threads and cording wools (Barbara Vidal)

It was decided for reasons of personal study that machine embroidery should be
the chosen medium, so various machine embroidery techniques were tried,
including vanishing fabric work, whipped stitch, inlay appliqué and quilting. The
fabrics and wools used are also included on this worksheet (Barbara Vidal)

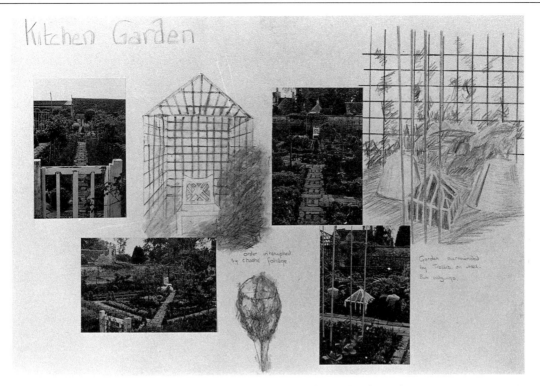

Kitchen Garden

order interrupted by chaotic foliage.

Garden surrounded by Trellis on wall. Box edging.

Kitchen garden. This worksheet, which includes photographs taken in the potager at Barnsley House, Gloucestershire, was the starting point of the investigation. The central idea evolved was that kitchen gardens were essentially trying to make (or keep) order out of chaos, and this became the theme (by the author)

Many photographs were taken in the kitchen garden at Barnsley House

Garden Path. A series of arches made by wrapping wire leading to a vanishing point is the main feature of this embroidery. The flowers and foliage were made by attaching small pieces of coloured transparent fabric and chiffons to the base. The path is hand stitched (Janet Bramwell)

RIGHT: Entrance, worked on dyed silk noile with a huge variety of threads and stitches. A human presence is indicated by use of a stumpwork basket (Sue Jones)

Worksheets used for different purposes may look slightly different and the approach may change. The following guidelines are meant to help in defining what the approach should be – what the first question is and how a design can be sought.

If the starting point is an image, there will be a gradual process to find out what is particularly of interest in that image, and how those points of interest can be described in textile form. The worksheets shown, on leaves, the water garden and the kitchen garden, all demonstrate this approach.

If an idea, notion or project title has been supplied, then researching images as well as deciding how to deal with them is necessary. The worksheets for this sort of problem can be exhaustive, as the images will first have to be understood or drawn and chosen before any textile work can be embarked upon. I include the series of worksheets that were done for the *Poetry Garden* in Chapter 7.

If a finished project is known or given – a bed quilt, jacket or accessory or any other item may be specifically required (the imagery to be used may even have been supplied in the case of a commission) – the worksheets must inquire into how a set of images can be turned into a solution for an object. The following

worksheets use drawings of lady's mantle and acer leaves as a starting point for a design for a complete bedroom.

The layout of a worksheet is important. Consider that writing normally works from left to right and from top to bottom, so if the worksheet is to be 'read' this format will work well. With experience, other layouts can be tried, but a starting point or focal point will always be required, so that the 'story' can be told from this point onwards. Make sure that the pattern of thought is made apparent by the layout chosen. Working in steps across and down the paper will create a more interesting worksheet than one that is simply worked in rows, but a rigid framework does help to clarify the order of the train of thought. Often many thoughts occur at once, so a worksheet that has no obvious pattern may seem more appropriate.

A paper should be chosen that will not cause any interference with the images, so white can be a good

The samples on this worksheet were all worked on beige felt, which was dyed in some instances. The background of the worksheet was quickly painted with the predominant theme of trellising. The samples were attached to become like views through the trellising.

Cotton print from dyed felt
Free machine + embroidery stitch

Satin stitch on dyed cotton
applique and vanishing fabric lace

Silk dyed with fibre tip dyes
Free machine embroidery

Silk dye on silk wadding
Free machine embroidery

Silk dyed with fibre-tip dyes - water added.
Free machine embroidery

Silk dye on silk wadding
Free machine - embroidery

Kitchen garden worksheet. The samples are as follows: cotton print from felt dyeing with free machine embroidery and embroidery using a set stitch (Bernina); satin stitch grid on dyed cotton with appliqué and vanishing fabric lace; silk dyed with fibre-tip dyes with free machine embroidery; silk dyes on silk wadding with free machine embroidery; silk dyed with fibre-tip dyes, then water added with free machine embroidery; silk dye on silk wadding with free machine embroidery

starting point. Fabrics, papers, and stitch samples may all be glued or stitched on to the paper; drawings in a variety of media may also become appropriate, so a heavy, smooth watercolour paper will probably be the most useful. I usually choose a 140 lb watercolour paper so that it will take whatever I decide to do, as what will happen next is not always predictable. The usual size for worksheets for commissions or competitions is A2, which provides enough space for a number of ideas to be laid out. If this is to be used, stretch a piece of paper larger than A2 and then draw the boundaries of an A2 size on to the paper, being careful to check the right-angles. My own preference is to work a full A1 size, as this allows me the space to really develop a set of ideas.

Samples can be made at any point in the process, and can be added to the worksheet. They can be mounted, or have a window mount cut in light card and placed over them (this can be appropriate if they are to be set apart from drawn images). For a less self-conscious or over-fussy approach, try overlocking, zigzagging or satin stitching around the edge of samples in a self-colour, or a colour that can form a border as well as fit in with an existing colour scheme. In some circumstances (when, perhaps, the drawings are particularly rough or moody) it may be appropriate to leave the edges as they are. Samples can be glued to the worksheet or fixed with double-sided tape, which is

more easily removed. They can also be stitched on – perhaps with a hand stitch at each corner, finished off neatly or left with a knot and a tassle. Don't think that once a needle has been picked up, drawing and working with art media can stop. The process of investigation will happen faster and more satisfactorily if creativity can occur in both art and textile media. Eventually there may be more textile than artwork, whereas at the start of the worksheets there may have been more artwork than textiles.

Colour swatches and 'shade cards' can be included in textiles and threads or in painted squares, which will help in the identification of colours required. Swatches may also be added to give textural or tonal information.

Wording and writing can often be a problem – just how much writing is necessary on a worksheet? As I have said, a worksheet should tell its own story and so a lot of writing will be unnecessary. That one image is disliked for certain reasons will become apparent as the

LEFT: **Courtyard in Greece 1**. Dyed fabrics are bonded to the ground. Stitching is by hand and machine. The tree is worked on vanishing fabric (Mary McQuade)

BELOW LEFT: **Courtyard in Greece 2**. Worked in bright colours to give an impression of heat. Embroidery on interlock canvas worked by hand and machine (Mary McQuade)

Gateway into a garden, worked as a sample for 'free Assisi work' on a dyed felt background (Eileen Bissell)

Archway and garden worked on silk dyed with wax resist. The archway and path are mounted separately to give a sense of depth. The embroidery is by machine. The leaves are worked on organdie and cut approximately to the stitching, giving a lightness of touch appropriate to the climbing plant (Sian Kibblewhite)

Poetry garden worksheet. The first worksheet includes writing to explain the notion of a poetry garden (see Chapter 8). Other writings are the 'sampling' of a Haiku. The progression of ideas for pavilions can be seen in the small sketches and large paintings. Small swatches of colour are included. This worksheet was done in watercolours by the author

On this worksheet the chosen pavilion is drawn, but in perspective as this was preferred on the previous sheet. Borders, backgrounds, and different colour ways are explored, including a stream and pool. The sampling of the Haiku continues (by the author)

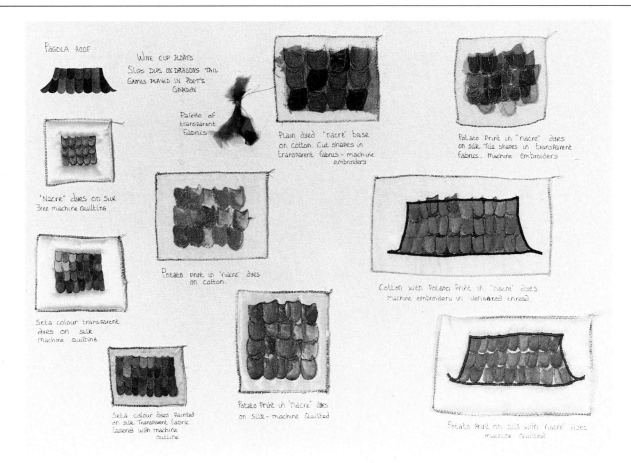

PAGOLA ROOF

WINE CUP FLOATS
SLIPS DIPS ON DRAGONS TAIL
GAMES PLAYED IN POET'S
GARDEN

Palette of
transparent
fabrics

Plain dyed "nacre" base
on cotton. Cut shapes in
transparent fabrics - machine
embroidery

Potato Print in "nacre" dyes
on silk. Tile shapes in transparent
fabrics. Machine embroidery

"Nacre" dyes on silk
free machine quilting

Potato print in "nacre" dyes
on cotton

Seta colour transparent
dyes on silk
machine quilting

Cotton with Potato Print in "nacre" dyes
machine embroidery in variegated thread.

Seta colour dyes painted
on silk. Transparent fabric
layered with machine
quilting

Potato Print in "nacre" dyes
on silk - machine Quilted

Potato Print on silk with "nacre" dyes
machine Quilted

This worksheet takes the pavilion roof as a starting point for embroidery
experiments (by the author)

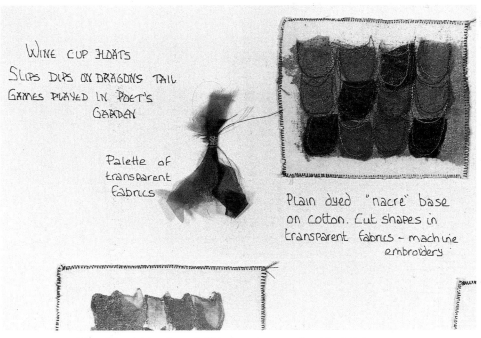

WINE CUP FLOATS
SLIPS DIPS ON DRAGONS TAIL
GAMES PLAYED IN POET'S
GARDEN

Palette of
transparent
fabrics

Plain dyed "nacre" base
on cotton. Cut shapes in
transparent fabrics - machine
embroidery

The potato print, layering and stitched samples are preferred for their freer
quality. The Haiku sampling continues

ABOVE LEFT: Final drawing developed from the poetry garden worksheets. Worked on a watercolour background with oil pastels (by the author)

ABOVE RIGHT: **Poetry Garden**. Worked on silk wadding with layered fabric and threads, dyeing and machine embroidery. The border is worked on vanishing fabric (by the author)

LEFT: Archway worked for the Chapter 7 project. The silk background is dyed with thinned dyes using pipettes, fingers, paintbrushes and a garden spray! The quilting is done by machine, mostly in whip stitch (by the author)

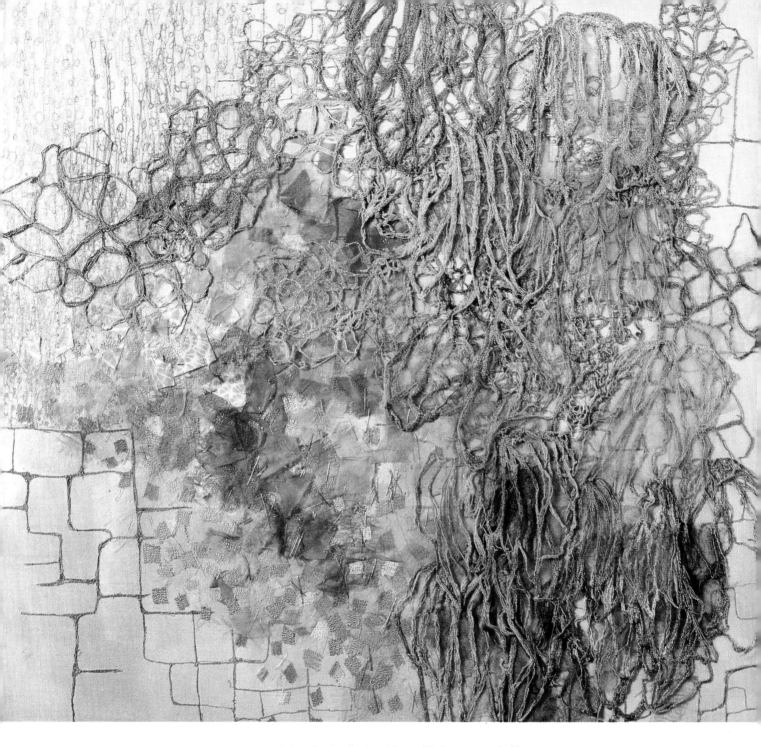

A Cotswold wall draped with aubretia and leaves. The leaves are worked by machine over chiffons on vanishing fabric. Chiffons and hand stitches are added to help mix the machine colours (Roma Edge)

next image is placed nearby with the 'dislikes' removed.

If an area is worthy of further investigation or sampling this does not have to be stated – the samples and further drawings or marks will speak for themselves. Writing may be important if descriptions of techniques are thought necessary so that they can be repeated at a later date. But phrases such as 'try doing this in dyeing and quilting' are virtually meaningless – how quilted, how stitched, how dyed? The dyed and quilted piece will show all that is necessary.

Numbering worksheets may seem appropriate so that the development of a train of thought from one sheet to the next becomes clear, but this can also be done by starting new worksheets with an image close to the last section of the previous sheet.

So keep words to a minimum – let the worksheet do the story-telling. Any wording that is used, however, should be done neatly and legibly (not too small), in a good hand or one that is appropriate to the image and notions about it – choose a suitable style of writing or do it in a comparable medium. If neat or clever writing is completely out of the question, try using rub-down lettering or a stencil, or develop a writing style by penning the letters against a ruler – a useful technique which also gives a straight line.

Often worksheets are done only when the embroidery is completed. A few samples and drawings are hastily put together for presentation purposes. The embroidery may have been unsuccessful in some way – the composition did not work, or the techniques or modes of presentation now seem ill thought out. This sort of dissatisfaction can even mean the non-completion of a piece that might have been worthy if only one or two changes in the design had been made. These would have become apparent through worksheeting. No effort or work is wasted when worksheeting. A vocabulary of techniques is gradually built up – a multitude of samples collected with only slight variations in theme or technique can be very informative. Compositional problems can be understood, or a variety of ideas for making boxes, hangings, pictures, garments, accessories or soft furnishings can be explored. This vocabulary will inform the process of worksheeting,

This final worksheet answered most of the remaining questions about how to work the embroidery and then construct the piece into a hanging. The hanging squares from each side of the pole are embroidered with each of the poems. The final piece is shown in the colour photograph on page 98

A set of three worksheets refer to a total bedroom design based on drawings from a small area of garden which included lady's mantle and an acer. In this worksheet an idea for a bed and valance is drawn with a curtain running down the side of the room to cover a bookshelf. Samples of fabric which may prove suitable and quilted leaves are included (Biddi Bennett)

The drawing represents an idea for a curtain pelmet. Samples are worked with quilting and metallic threads worked by hand and machine, and samples on organza with dyeing and machine embroidery (Biddi Bennett)

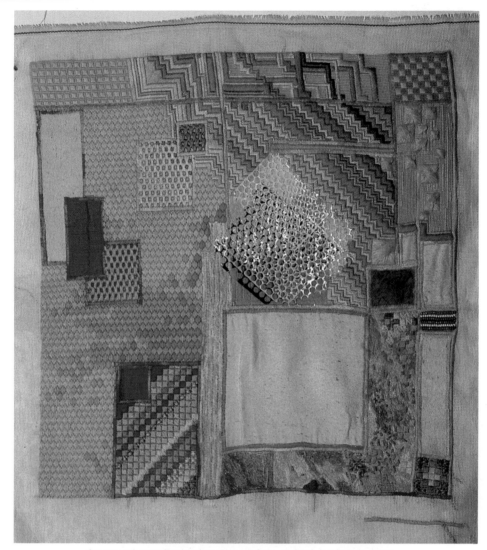

Canvas work using hand and machine stitchery, appliqué, beads and sequin waste. Various types of garden are represented including knot gardens, paving, carpet bedding, a wild garden, walled gardens and a Japanese stone garden. Worked on a lockweave canvas to avoid pulling problems (by the author)

This embroidery was worked by drawing directly onto an etching plate and using this to print on to the fabric which was already layered. Additional embroidery is then included (Claire Williams)

Embroidery worked on a dyed synthetic silky fabric that included some potato printing. Machine cording of wools was included with machine embroidery. This may not be the final piece, as larger and three-dimensional pieces have also been suggested (Barbara Vidal)

Secret Garden. Worked by machine on a grey silk ground. The whole piece was quilted, then the backing and wadding removed from the area to receive the heavy embroidery. The embroidery was worked using many different tensions. I wrote the words for the piece, which are as follows: 'In my secret garden, Colour riots from fertile source, Opens out in heat of day, And wild dreams seed there.' (by the author)

sampling and decision-making the next time – certain answers to questions may be known to be unsatisfactory, others worth a try.

Worksheets and samples, done seriously and not rushed, will improve the final embroidery enormously. They do not take a long time, when compared with how long some pieces of embroidery can take, and indeed can save time in the long run as the embroidery embarked upon can be more satisfactory from the start. As this method of finding original and personal methods of embroidery and design is pursued, the nature of the worksheets themselves may also take on

aspects that are individual – ideas and trains of thought may be joined up with great sweeps of watercolour washed on; or borders may be included that relate to the designs; the method of attaching samples may acquire a very personal style, or any writing could make use of an interest in calligraphy. The worksheets themselves will begin to take on the themes of the images and the style of the design. The ideas that affect the worksheet will be an influence throughout the embroidery, which will consequently become coherent and well-informed, and more satisfying as a completed piece.

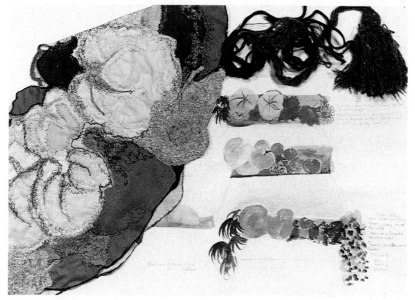

Three drawings represent different ideas for a headboard design. Colours of wool and a tassel are included. The large sample worked with appliqué, machine and hand embroidery was worked for a lampshade (Biddi Bennett)

7

FROM START TO FINISH

TRANSLATING an image into embroidery is something that many people are fearful of. Choosing an image and deciding how to work it often seems a daunting task, but this need not be so. In Chapter 6 I detailed how worksheets and samples would help to overcome this stumbling block – one way or another, a method of embroidery will become apparent.

In this chapter I aim to show how an image can be used to create many different styles of embroidery. Both of the images used here are taken from the garden at Dragon House, Chipping Campden, which is open to the public in aid of charity. In each image, a number of students volunteered to work a picture in a style which currently interested them.

The entrance to the garden

The archway constructed from a tree was a good image. Depth was created by the effect of a distance that could not be completely seen. The steps and path took the viewer into the picture, whilst the flower pots on each side had a welcoming effect. The framework that the tree provided made this a perfect image. The major difficulty was experienced in the rendition of the warm red bush in the middle distance, which had the effect of flattening this creation of depth – this became a problem in all of the embroideries and one which was dealt with in different ways.

The working of the embroidery helped each student to learn to deal with depth and certain aspects of perspective and colour work associated with its creation. They were also able to take the techniques that interested them a little further in these embroideries.

My own embroidery on this theme (colour photograph on page 00) was dyed directly on to habutai silks using pipetted and fibre-tip refill dyes. Thus a very loose image was inevitable, as the dye is runny and bleeds well on silk. I also used my fingers and a garden water spray – the tree to the right was streaked using my finger nails! The final result has all the immediacy of any watercolour painting done *in situ*. The machine embroidery and quilting serves to 'tidy' some areas and cause further disarray in others.

Border with stream

The second image was slightly more difficult – an area of border with a stream running through it and including a small waterfall. The image itself was a little less interesting, having no framework and no real focal point. However, because of this, the embroiderers had to find more in their own work to hold the interest, and the stitching in the following pieces shows some innovation.

RIGHT: Embroidery worked from the painting on page 108, showing a liveliness gained from the knowledge learned in painting direct from life, as opposed to the confines of a photographic image. Worked by hand and machine, much on vanishing muslin laid on the surface. The silk noile base is dyed roughly to indicate certain areas. Appliqué and shadow work are included in the steps and paving. Hand stitches mixed into machined areas change the scale and offer textural interest. The red bush proved difficult, and was only resolved after much reworking. The quality of the unfinished painted edge is maintained in the presentation of the embroidery (Mary McQuade)

LEFT: Janet Bramwell's first creative embroidery is seen on page 37. Her meticulous stitchery is very suitable for creating effective stumpwork, the technique she chose for this panel worked for the chapter 7 project. The feeling of depth created by the image itself is further emphasised by the raised technique, and even became the subject of a visual joke in her treatment of the foreground pavement, which leaves the picture plane and leans towards the viewer at an angle of about 30 degrees. The background was worked entirely in hand stitching, with machine embroidery included gradually as its fineness appealed and it proved appropriate. The problem of the red bush became evident again, but the flatness of the stitchery in comparison to the foreground and the inclusion of dark blues and greens helped to keep the bush in the distance.

BELOW: Garden worked on canvas and handmade felt with hand stitchery (Maggie Shaw)

RIGHT: Panel worked entirely in écru coloured threads which vary from fine to coarse silks and cottons and some synthetics: beads and sequins are also added. Stitches include chain, stem, long-legged cross, fly, satin, padded satin, button-hole wheels and french knots (Di Chester)

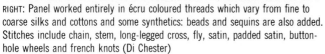

ABOVE RIGHT: The photograph was photocopied and enlarged to provide a scaled-up image for two of the embroideries. The photocopy itself proved inspirational. It suggested that the textures involved might be suitable for a one-colour embroidery – and so the white work and then gold work pieces were designed; and it also suggested a more 'blurred' way of seeing this rigid photographic image – thus I decided to dye my embroidery very loosely and maintain a 'blurred' quality (see page 107)

A painting worked on stretched cartridge paper in gouache paints. Washes and thicker areas of paint were used (Mary McQuade)

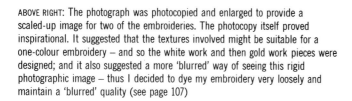

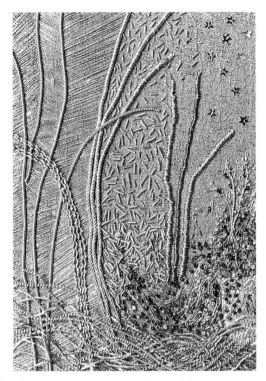

A gold work piece concentrating on a small area of the monotonal embroidery. The photograph is not referred to, but instead the white work becomes a source of inspiration. The area under scrutiny includes the right-hand flower pot and part of the tree. This area was chosen by moving two L-shaped pieces of card around until a suitable texture area was found. Di Chester was already familiar with gold work and chose to do this piece as a way of tackling something a little freer. The gold work uses 'ordinary' embroidery stitches worked in lustred threads, as well as couched jap gold and pearl purl, with beads and pearls used for seeding

This close-up of the left-hand side of the picture worked by Janet Bramwell shows the stitch and construction techniques. The wall and pavement are 'patched' together with card shapes covered in dyed fabric. The wall is draped with ivy which is worked on vanishing fabric. The fuchsia and lobelia were also worked on vanishing fabric and applied. The steps are made of ten individually cut pieces of card, each covered in dyed fabric and then stuck together. The handrail is constructed from wire and then wrapped with pearl cottons (Janet Bramwell)

LEFT: Having explored the image thoroughly in tones, a large coloured piece was started — this piece is A1! Many different threads are used, including ribbons and cords and knitting yarns. Fibre-tips, crayons and dyes are used for colouring the background where necessary. The background fabric is a strong linen painter's canvas. The area chosen for the gold work piece was again used, but a drawing was worked first to define the colours, as the photograph could not give detailed enough information (Di Chester)

Lace garden worked on hot-water-soluble fabric by machine. The bobbin was changed each time the top thread was changed so that the lace is the same back and front (by the author)

RIGHT: Hand and machine embroidery on an interlock canvas, showing a small area of garden. Texture and stitching details are heightened by the use of machine stitchery over large hand stitches and vice versa (Audrey Butt)

These close-ups show areas of stitchery from the bottom of page 109

This close-up shows the background of hand-stitched seeding, straight stitch and knots. The tree trunk is satin stitch worked in various thicknesses of pearl thread over cord. The leaves on the tree are worked on vanishing fabric, as are the contents of the flower pot which are padded. The flower pot is dyed and padded silk. The leaves of the hosta at the base of the tree are worked with needlemade lace over wire. The strands of bush coming into the picture were worked on individual pieces of wire placed on vanishing fabric. The foreground flowers were created by working circles on vanishing fabric which were then folded in half and made into S-shapes. Two of these form each flower – this is a technique used for forming flowers in cake icing! The leaves are made on vanishing fabric and then gathered at the base using wrapped wire. The flowers and leaves are wired as would be done for a corsage or buttonhole, and then attached to a background of machine embroidery on vanishing fabric (Janet Bramwell)

Embroidery worked on silk noile. The photocopy was used to make a direct drawing on to the silk. The picture was then carefully painted with fabric dyes used straight out of the pot to avoid any 'bleeding'. Worked by an embroiderer who always dyes carefully, but often covers the dyeing completely with stitching; it was decided to keep the stitchery to a minimum so that the dyeing could become a major aspect of this picture. The stitchery was kept simple and used to pick out foreground detail; there is less stitching as the image recedes. The difficult red bush was dealt with by adding cooler shades to its base, and the fact that it is not stitched at all also keeps it in the distance (Sheila Barrow)

Detail from the embroidery in the colour photograph on page 110 showing the stitchery worked in wools, pearl cottons, soft embroidery cottons, thick synthetics, and ribbons. The background fabric is dyed, the water is layers of see-through fabrics with stitching in stranded threads and silver. The foreground leaves are based on straight or satin stitches worked in shiny and matt threads (Sue Jones)

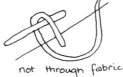
not through fabric

not through fabric

not through fabric

not through fabric

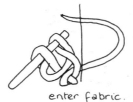
enter fabric.

Single knotted diamond stitch. This stitch is neater, bulkier and easier than a french knot if ribbon is to be used, as in the embroideries on pages 91 and 110

ABOVE: **Red Border**. Worked on a dyed silk ground entirely by machine using a straight stitch with free machine embroidery (Roma Edge)

BELOW LEFT: **Cottage with two cats**. Worked by hand on dyed silk noile (Sheila Barrow)

ABOVE LEFT: The background of silk is dyed with fibre-tip dyes and machine quilted (Gloria Jenkins)

RIGHT: **Border**. Stitched on a dyed ground using a variety of threads, including ribbon (Roma Edge)

Design from the worksheet opposite worked on hot water (or more correctly, boiling water) soluble fabric with white rayon machine embroidery thread. The net areas of poppy seed heads are applied. The area around them worked with vertical and horizontal lines (weave stitch). The poppy leaves are solid zigzag; the lower leaf shapes are worked with a three-step zigzag, interlocking at the points. Circles are drawn for the other flowers, and the water is represented by long double lines of stitching with 'bubbles' used to interconnect. All stitching is worked freely on a sewing machine (by the author)

Detail focusing on the layers of straight stitch worked in wool for the coarse leaves. The poppy heads are padded satin stitch and the leaves are satin stitch worked in a deliberately 'rough' manner. The foreground is a base of fly stitch with blocks of buttonhole stitch over. The area to the left has a base of straight vertical stitches in pearl cottons with a single knotted diamond stitch worked in ribbon. The background is worked with a stalked french knot. The thread is brought through the fabric, but the knot is made and the needle passed back through the fabric at a distance from this original point, leaving a straight stitch before the knot (Sue Jones)

RIGHT: A drawing with oil pastels preceded this embroidery and was used for the source material instead of the photograph. The silk noile background fabric was first dyed. Coloured scrims were then stitched with a zigzag in a hoop on the sewing machine to create a pulled work surface texture, which was then stitched to the background fabric. Further stitching was then added by machine to create a highly textured surface uncharacteristic of much machine embroidery (Gloria Jenkins)

RIGHT: Embroidery worked on dyed silk noile in stranded cottons using a variety of stitches including padded satin, straight, stem, french knots and seeding (Sheila Barrow)

BELOW: A quick worksheet started with a drawing of a section of the photograph to investigate shape. From this the idea for a cutwork or lacework panel was evolved. Possible ideas for hanging the embroidery were also included on the worksheet (by the author)

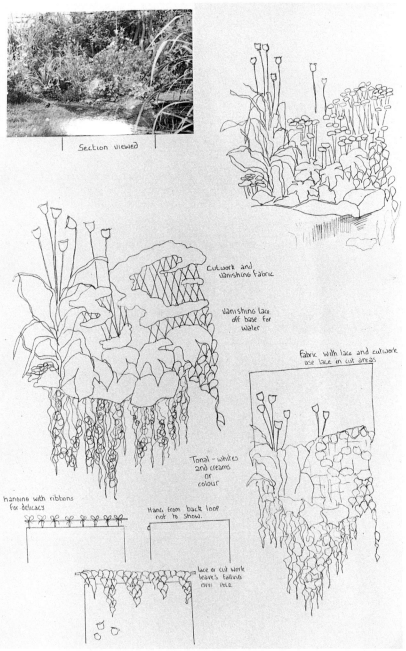

Section viewed

Cutwork and vanishing fabric

Vanishing lace off base for water

Fabric with lace and cutwork use lace in cut areas

Tonal – whites and creams or colour

hanging with ribbons for delicacy

Hang from back loop not to show.

lace or cut work leaves falling over pole

Wild flowers form this 'garden' scene embroidered from photographs taken in Greece. The embroidery is worked both by hand and machine, including work on vanishing fabric to create additional texture (Mary McQuade)

GARDENS IN EMBROIDERY

*'Learning from books and teachers is like travelling by
carriage, but the carriage will serve only while one is on the
highroad. He who reaches the end of the highroad
will leave the carriage and walk afoot.'*

Quoted in Johannes Itten, *The Elements of Colour*, 1961

Entrances

The feeling or mood of a garden can be created even
before it is entered. The entrance to a garden can
indicate whether it will be neat or wild, cool or hot,
ramshackle or ordered, friendly or distant. Entrances
can be made with gates in walls, fences or hedges;
archways created out of trees, climbing plants and
flowers on supports, or wooden or metal structures;
gates may be simple or ornate. Pathways will lead into
the garden or up to a door; through to an unseen view
where there may be peace and quiet; or perhaps down
a long vista where the beauties of the garden reveal
themselves all at once.

Entrances to gardens worked in embroidery can
reflect all of these things, and any textile medium may
be suitable. Three-dimensional techniques often spring
to mind because of the qualities of depth that entrances
can give. But as depth can be drawn using various
techniques, it can also be stitched with similar methods
of fading colour and detail, or using perspective; thus
entrances can be worked to good effect in two- as well
as three-dimensional embroidery.

Entrances with doors that lead nowhere visible
require little creation of depth and can be worked in
very free techniques, creating an illusion of an opening
instead of absolute realism.

The natural garden

Old accounts of idyllic unattended gardens abound in
the legends of almost every culture from the Christian
Garden of Eden to the Greek myths.

The Garden of Eden, more than anything, represents
man's inability to accept even the most beautiful things
as they are – he has to experiment and change and
thus eventually loses all. Of course, in Eden (as with
Pandora), Eve can be held to blame!

The quality of a natural garden is always bittersweet.
It is inevitably transient – the flowers will fade quickly,
and as soon as it is discovered it will change. Yet in
mythology these spaces are idyllically created, perhaps
by a benevolent God for the use of a favoured human.
The trees part to reveal a grassy glade, perhaps on an
island or in a forest. The grass is rich with flowers, a
stream is full of leaping fish and the trees are heavy
with fruit. Once here, labour is unnecessary – all the
food ever desired is at hand.

There is still a thrill in finding an area of hedgerow
ripe with wild blackberries; a quiet field full of wild

Entrance to a Secret Garden. An unfinished embroidery worked on dyed silk noile with appliqué, hand stitching in stranded cottons and flower threads, and some beads (by the author)

mushrooms; hedgerows or grass verges alive with the colour of wild flowers; poppies lending colour to a field of wheat seen through a tumbledown wall from a verge filled with cow parsley or ragged robin; a clearing in a wood giving way to a scene of crowded bluebells or cowslips; a heathered moor or a real wild alpine garden. Wild and natural gardens can be found, and are more recently being created within cultivated gardens. They offer a delicacy of flower form that is not always found in cultivated gardens. The shapes and forms of the flowers may be clearly defined; or flowers scattered through the grass are redolent of a medieval tapestry; in a bluebell wood the calm, blue carpet-like appearance will be broken only by trees and odd leaf shapes or blades of grass peeping through.

Natural gardens can be calming and reassuring, giving a feeling of nature in control, but charmingly so. Embroideries of such subjects often reflect the delight to be found in such scenes, but this delight might change to uneasiness when the darker side of nature takes control and the beauty fades.

The retreat

The notion of a countryside retreat to get away from the grime, pace and pressures of the city is not new. In AD 360 Emperor Julian had such a retreat where he would relax and worship.

Having a retreat out of the city in times of plague was the province of the rich, but thought essential, and

Silk dyes on silk using resist technique. This was then quilted. The quilt wadding and background fabric were removed from the central areas which were then embroidered. I wrote the poem **A Unicorn Tapestry** in response to a poem by Leonard Cohen. It is about the search for perfect love, embodied in the myth of the unicorn and the virgin. The words are written around the outside of each embroidery and are as follows:

'You entered the grove
Summer hot with promise,
And gently the blue carpet
Gave way to the unicorn trail.

You stayed in the grove,
But no myth could you capture,
The love of virgin souls
Rests darkly on the shaded bracken.'

Guildford Castle Gardens. Worked on a background of fabric-painted felt with hand and machine embroidery and small areas of appliqué (Sonya Head)

Beauty in Dereliction. The idea for this hanging came from a photograph of derelict mills in Halifax with a foreground of willow herb, coupled with an idea taken from the Arts and Crafts Movement where an image flowed through a number of ceramic tiles. The space-dyed ground has applied gauzes and chiffons with mainly hand embroidery. The 'tiles' are mounted on wood with dupion covered cardboard frames (Margaret Kimberley)

was a practice provided for until the last century. But a retreat can be found anywhere – in an area of green plants in a room overlooking a city; an enclosed 'pocket handkerchief' garden, beautifully planted, smelling sweetly and perhaps with a small pool; or perhaps an area of dereliction grows with wild flowers and becomes a garden retreat for insects and animals as well as humans.

A retreat may be small or park sized, but the impact created on all the senses can be difficult to portray in a purely visual medium. Embroideries can be created that have sound and smell – hanging tassels with glass or ceramic beads, or pieces of shisha, could make noises which inspire the notion of water splashing; pot pourri could be included to give garden smells to a hanging. A feeling of quietude and rest can be implied by the colours used or the calmness of the stitching or technique employed. Cool colours will give a better feeling of rest than hot colours: expanses of colour rather than busy areas of intense texture may increase this effect. But highly textured and busy areas may offer the notion of a wildness and bustle, an area of

Garden. Worked mainly by machine on to a dyed ground with added chiffons and hand stitching (Roma Edge)

RIGHT: Machine embroidery on silk, worked from a pencil crayon drawing. The leaves hanging from the cutwork greenery at the bottom of the garden are worked on vanishing fabric. The backing shows at the base of the embroidery as a foil to the lace leaves (Roma Edge)

intense interest against a bland city background.

A favourite retreat can come alive in a restful piece of embroidery, or a colourful piece of stitchery can create a place in which to become lost from the pressures of the city.

The enclosed courtyard garden

'Paradise' comes from the Persian word 'Pairidaeza', meaning enclosure, and was originally applied to an enclosed hunting park that was owned by the King, but eventually came to mean an enclosed cultivated garden of a variety of proportions, where a king or ruler would be safe and could rest in peaceful tranquillity.

These cultivated enclosed gardens featured orderly planting, and included fruits, scents and flowers. Evergreens were important for year-round colour, as the habit of deciduous shrubs and trees was redolent of death and the old.

A garden can give experiences other than the merely visual. The scent of beautiful blossoms and the sound of running water or the light splash of a fountain are all important to the enclosed garden, and ways of expressing these may become important to an embroidery – look at the section on retreats, above.

The medieval square or rectangular cloister made a perfect enclosure within which to make a garden. Such a garden would be split geometrically with crossing paths and areas of fruit, or more often just herbs. Vegetables were not included, as these would be grown out in the fields. Flowers were a luxury in early gardens, where herbs predominated for culinary and medicinal use.

The patio garden offers a modern version of a closed or semi-closed garden structure. It takes as its model the old cloisters and the outdoor rooms and courtyards used as living and eating spaces in warm countries. The patio garden can offer many features and textures that can be inspiring for an embroiderer, particularly when set against the order and neatness associated with these areas. Contrasting stonework, brickwork or paving with plants growing in paving gaps, up walls or in pots can offer a design source for many embroidery techniques. People, or objects which indicate the presence of people, such as tables and chairs or food, could also be included in such an embroidery.

Cloisters with statues and fountains can offer a challenge to the more experienced embroiderer where space, depth of field and perspective will have to be dealt with.

The patterns created by enclosed gardens can also be a starting point for embroideries. The formal pattern of Islamic courtyards offers a point of solace or meditation.

The secret garden

Artificially enclosed gardens, with walls, trees and other natural devices, have often been created within larger gardens. The *Giardino Segreto* or secret garden is a feature of many Italian Renaissance gardens. These gardens were hidden or discreetly tucked away. The extent of their privacy varies – some are by no means secret at all, but the intention is the same: to provide an intimate area where garden and water delights may be enjoyed away from the full gaze of other visitors.

Enclosed gardens were associated with the Virgin Mary, who is often depicted within the confines of a walled garden. In Solomon's 'Song of Songs' it says 'A garden enclosed is my sister, my spouse, a spring shut up, a fountain sealed'. Thus an enclosed garden was associated with purity and virginity, a protective wall around a chaste woman. Secret gardens have long been symbols of women's sexuality – to protect purity, or as a secret place of pleasure and discovery.

Secret gardens continue to fascinate – there is a certain excitement and pleasure in discovering the apparently undiscovered. Secret gardens still exist in some preserved Italian gardens, and there is an Italian-style secret garden at St Paul's Walden Bury in Hertfordshire.

Knots, parterres, mazes and herbs

The sixteenth century is characterised by a love of fantasy, puzzlement and obscurity; the use of double meaning and intricacy in design and execution, broadly termed 'conceits'.

The elaborations of the knot garden epitomise this interest. The knot was an ornamental garden bed, laid out within an enclosed garden, with patterns of low evergreen bushes and gaps between them laid out with flowers or herbs, or with coloured materials such as sand or brickdust. The framework of the designs was usually made of scented herbs and if the garden was of any size it would usually be divided into groups planted for 'nosegay' use, and those for culinary and medicinal purposes.

The knot was usually set within a square framework. Sometimes one type of flower would occupy each area or corresponding pattern areas; sometimes the infill of herbs and flowers was quite indiscriminate. The most intricate patterns usually only contained coloured sands and materials, as such designs were difficult to maintain neatly if additional herbs or flowers were present. Interwoven patterns of embroidered or 'strap' work were made by planting contrasting threads of lines of different plants – a closed knot. A simpler design without interwoven lines and with the square merely divided into sections was called an open knot.

Islamic Pool. This embroidery worked by quilting on to silk dyed with pearlised dyes is framed with a ceramic tile made of 'raku' fired 'T' material clay. This is a ceramic technique that involves taking the tile out of the kiln whilst red hot and plunging it into sawdust to obtain reductions and smoking effects (by the author)

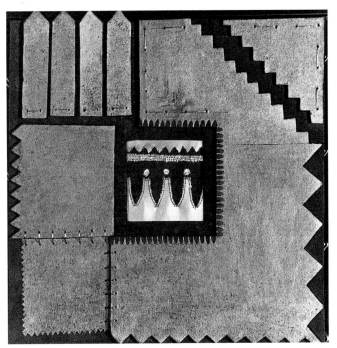

Courtyard. The central embroidery is worked by applying gold paper to a rich burgundy silk ground. The frame is made of 'raku' fired 'T' material clay. The frame itself is made of layers of slabs of clay. The top layer is cut into the pattern and has lustres applied. Holes are made before firing so that stitches may be added when the processes are complete (by the author)

Knot Garden. Worked on a dyed silk background with a silk covered cut mount. The embroidery is by hand and machine and includes metallic threads and ribbons (Iris Eyles)

Porcelain tiles made as frames for embroidery. Holes are made when the clay is 'green' for stitchery when the work is complete. The top tile is worked by hand with added machine whip stitch. The lower one is worked in cross stitch and stalked french knots only (by the author)

Winter Garden. Worked on silk noile with a sort of Italian quilting that was stuffed as work progressed. Hand embroidered with beads (Sonya Head)

The knots used became a symbol of status – the more complicated the knot, the more wealthy the owner, as more time could be afforded for its inception and upkeep. The most prized knots were those most similar to the embroidery they were trying to emulate.

Knot garden designs copied patterns on leatherwork, plasterwork, tiles and wood panelling, but the most popular designs came from embroidery. There was a desire to achieve perfection, which showed that the gardener or owner had nature controlled within the boundaries of the garden wall, and this implied a sense of control over the surroundings.

While it is true that knot gardens were inspired by embroidery, such gardens were also influential in design and embroidery. Knot gardens are still a popular starting point for design, offering patterns and order in which colour and texture can be controlled.

The word 'parterre', which means on or along the ground, literally 'by earth', was first used in the mid-sixteenth century when it became interchangeable with the word 'garden'. It came to mean a regular or foursquare garden or a garden where the beds were well-ordered, but as the desire for ever more complicated patterns and knot designs increased, the nature of the garden changed. In French gardens intricate knot designs included designs of letters, patterns, figures, beasts, coats-of-arms, buildings and boats. Many different herbs were used to create the parterre, but for longevity and ease of use box was eventually preferred. Parterres, unlike knot gardens, became gardens to be looked at from a distance rather than wandered through, and this meant that smells (many people dislike the smell of box) became unimportant.

Designs increased in scale, being complicated near the house or viewing terrace and simpler further away, and so notions of perspective became involved in their creation and design. The designer of the garden became paramount, and designs emulated embroidery and weaving to create textile effects known as 'parterres de broderie'.

Whereas knots had been features in isolation, often bearing little relation to their neighbours, the new schemes were a unified whole that related to the house and its view and were now symmetrical.

Historically, parterres do not contain flowers, so for the embroiderer they have relevance as strong pattern only. There are good examples of restored parterres in

Summer Garden. The knots of the winter garden lift up to reveal the summer garden. The tree and pool are reversed (Sonya Head)

Europe, at Augustusburg at Brühl in Germany, and at the Papal residence of Castelgandolfo. In England there is a formal 'parterre d'eau' built in this century by Achille Duchêne at Blenheim Palace in Oxfordshire, which, because of its mixture of box hedging, gravel, stone, water and statues may offer a better starting point for embroidery.

Mazes and puzzles are closely related in technique and design to knot gardens and parterres, which were popular when mazes came into being as a garden ornament in the late fifteenth century. They can offer structure and intrigue to an embroidery just as much as to a garden.

There are mazes at Hampton Court in Surrey, Chatsworth in Derbyshire, and Hatfield House in Hertfordshire. All these later mazes are of full height and are not sweet smelling. Perhaps the desire is for the fun and fear of Alice in Wonderland, but there is something special in the 'Renaissance conceit' of being lost in a maze that is less than knee high.

Embroideries on the theme of a maze need to consider pattern, but perhaps also contain the notion of something searched for at the centre of the maze – perhaps some goal, as in Greek mythology, or else simple peace and quiet or something more spiritual. Bearing in mind the use of fragrant plants for the mazes of the Renaissance, perhaps the embroidery could relate to a pot pourri, or even contain one within the design.

Herb gardens are still created today within frameworks to prevent the garden being overrun – frameworks can be made of paving and brick as well as hedging. Recently herbs are invading the flower border, offering usefulness as well as scent to the garden.

This notion of being overrun can affect a drawing of knots and parterres if the restraints present within the design are allowed to be overrun with the colours and textures of the plants present. This idea can inform an embroidery, whether worked with the machine with dyed areas, or whether the restraint of the knot is detailed by appliqué or canvas work with additional stitching breaking into the pattern and causing interest with colour and texture.

Municipal parks and carpet bedding

Carpet bedding was, perhaps, the natural Victorian reaction to the excesses of the landscape gardens of the preceding century. The dawning of suburbia, middle-class home owners with small gardens, and the creation of more regulated and often smaller municipal parks, meant that a new thinking in garden design was necessary. The new middle class did not want unruly cottage gardens, and the increase in availability of different plant and flower types, as well as the

invention of the lawnmower, meant that an orderly lawn and flower garden was now within the reach of anyone with a small plot.

The understanding of the needs of plants led to the creation of large greenhouses in which huge quantities of annuals could be raised for the carpet bedding. Characteristic of such bedding is the circular bed which rises up in a 'wedding cake' design, with low plants on the outside, gradually increasing in size to a showy plant in the centre.

Victoria Park in London still retains outstanding areas of carpet bedding faithful to nineteenth-century principles. The relationship between these beds and the canvas work and ribbon work of the period is clear, but it is often difficult to think of contemporary uses for such designs. The colour photographs on page 102 include some areas related to bedding, and also show a charming view of a municipal park.

Cottage gardens and herbaceous borders

The cottage garden style, which came into its own in the nineteenth century, was a decorative but practical blending of the small-scale mixed plantings of the rural cottager and the formal garden. Lawns were not generally used in smaller gardens because they were difficult to keep neatly cropped until the lawnmower became widely available. It was therefore less work to have a garden bulging with flowers, herbs and vegetables alongside pathways in brick or gravel, than to have large lawns covering most of the garden plot, which is the current fashion and which allows for less intensive gardening.

The true cottage garden had paths edged with low hedges, usually of box, but sometimes of lavender or cotton lavender, or even of trained fruit bushes. Within the hedges flowers, fruit and vegetables were planted together. The most useful herbs might be planted near the kitchen door, and fragrant flowers such as honeysuckle, climbing roses or lilies, would be placed by windows. This was a garden for practicality and pleasure.

The nineteenth century was concerned with the picturesque qualities associated with rural life, and the ideal life of the cottager was a popular subject of art and literature, even though it was a little misconceived. Even in the twentieth century this rural idyll has been more than adequately represented in embroideries of cottages, cottage gardens and crinolined ladies. However, cottage gardens, with their wealth of shape and colour contrasting against windows, doors and pavements, can still make interesting and new compositions for embroidery.

Herbaceous borders largely developed from cottage gardens, but created a more tidy and manageable form

Observing the Garden. Worked with tiny pieces of dyed fabric, stitched down to represent the brush marks in the original design. The padded figure was taken from a statue at Alton Towers. Stitching is done by hand with machine cottons and rayons, and tapestry silks (Belinda Downes)

My First Garden. Completed from a series of garden paintings on a long narrow format, views are patchworked together into an embroidery which is worked with padding and hand embroidery, including detached buttonhole (Belinda Downes)

Snowshill Summer, using padding and hand embroidery. The figure was taken from a garden in Woodhouse Eaves, from Snowshill in Gloucestershire (Belinda Downes)

as borders to walkways – paved, gravelled or grassed. The herbaceous border was most often contained within a rectangular format with a wall or hedge to give it a vertical backing. It generally contained perennial plants, although there may have been space for a small mix of annuals, and it marks the beginning of floral informality in garden design, which is now well represented in mixed as well as in herbaceous borders. The importance of plants is paramount in these gardens: colour, foliage and shape all play a part, with a floral display that lasts as long as possible. These are beneficial to anyone approaching drawing and design work with a view to embroidery. The earliest surviving example of an herbaceous border is at Arley Hall in Cheshire, where a double border has been maintained according to a plan dated 1846. Arley Hall also boasts a scented garden, a walled herb garden and a fish garden.

Towards the end of the nineteenth century the herbaceous border came under the more subtle influence of Gertrude Jekyll. She pioneered the notion of making tonal and harmoniously coloured gardens. Colour was moderate, and heavy-headed show blooms were considered out of place. Gardens such as those at Hidcote in Gloucestershire and Sissinghurst in Kent are good examples of the style advocated by Jekyll. The structure is provided by walls and hedges, walkways and garden buildings. The garden is divided into compartments containing attractive displays which may be seasonal, harmonious in colour, contrasting or tonal, or work on a theme of shape or mood.

All such gardens are an excellent source of inspiration. The notion of having separate views hedged into individual gardens is useful for someone who is still trying to draw everything seen. The privacy that such gardens can afford can also be an attraction for the novice still nervous about drawing in too public a place. Also in such a garden there is bound to be something of interest that will be useful for any project.

Giverny

Perhaps one of the most famous gardens in the art world is that at Giverny, close to Vernon, on the Seine. Claude Monet moved to Giverny in 1883, and he lived there, with occasional interludes, for over forty years, during which time he painted scenes in and around the garden.

Part of his garden was arranged in a geometrical fashion, but much of it is 'wild' in the manner of the more 'avant garde' gardens of the time, with no

Border with Wall. Worked on a dyed background in hand embroidery (Roma Edge)

RIGHT: **View.** Fabric paint with couched threads and knots, fly stitch, chain stitch and straight stitch (Sonya Head)

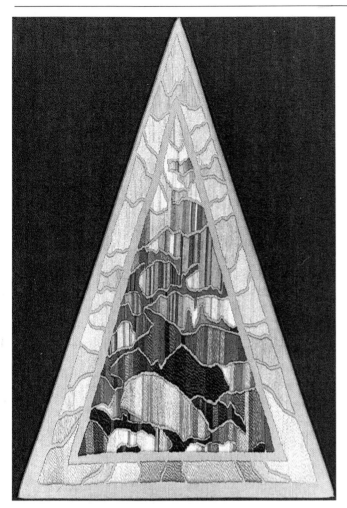

Border. Worked with straight stitches, the strong diagonals and the fading colours give this embroidery its quality of a view receding into the distance (April Tremlette)

Close-up of **Poetry garden** Sample. Worked on silk wadding with trapped threads under a layer of see-through fabrics. The silk wadding was dyed with silk dyes (by the author)

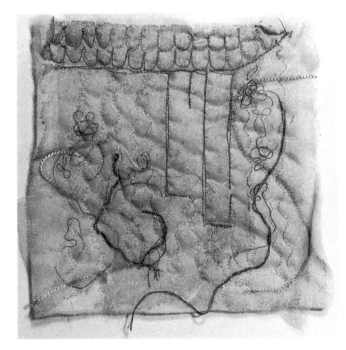

If only we could meet here. Worked on old lace over a silk ground. The hollyhocks and leaves are drawn with free machine embroidery. The lace curtain through which the view is seen is worked on vanishing muslin. The words are stitched by machine in the centre of the flowers (by the author)

Pot. The padded and stitched silk base contains leaves and flowers applied with 'bondaweb' and some hand stitching (Sonya Head)

The poet's garden

For the Chinese, a garden without poetry would seem incomplete. Their literature and garden history testify to the concept of the two being somehow inseparable – gardens were intended to inspire poetry. This notion spread to Japan, and both the Chinese and Japanese built pavilions which contained streams which wound around and through them in a dragon's-tail design. A cup of wine was floated on the stream, and in the time it took to pass through the pavilion a poem had to be composed – a game which has a long history in Chinese and Japanese garden design.

The tradition continues today in Japan, where competitions for the composing of Haiku poems still take place in the pavilion in Koraku-en Garden in Okoyama.

The notion of using one or two words to help concentrate the mind on the essential properties of the garden has already been discussed. The use of a poem, or a few lines from one, may also be a good starting point for an embroidered image, whether those lines are chosen from a poem or written by the embroiderer about the image or its moods. Poetry is traditional on samplers, but its potential for use with other forms of embroidery has largely been ignored.

Sculpture and ornament in gardens

Sculpture has long been used to add interest and form to gardens. From Classical times to the present, sculpture has often been included, sometimes designed for a specific garden. Sculpture was popular on an heroic scale in all gardens which attempted to emulate

restrictions or artificial constraints. It is unusual for such a garden to survive – this is no doubt due to Monet's own fame. The structures that exist in the garden, such as the bridges over the artificial lake and the rose arches, are so overgrown with plants (and were for most of Monet's years at Giverny) that the artificiality is drowned under the colour and disarray that nature has to offer.

The plants themselves become the centre of interest, since their shapes and colours are valued above any architectural qualities of the garden. It is these colours, formulated around a loose structure, that occupied many of Monet's paintings when he was not obsessed with reflections and water lilies.

Monet's gardens at Giverny are a riot of colour and as such offer an excellent starting point for embroideries on this theme. The use of colour is unusual: in Britain more subtlety is expected, and it is this that can be so enlightening to the artist, embroiderer and garden designer! Created for an artist, they are an artist's dream. Examples of drawings and embroideries from Giverny can be seen in the colour photographs on pages 70, 74 and 75.

Pot. Worked on canvas with a variety of stitches in stranded cottons (Beryl Higson)

the Italian Renaissance style, and in later gardens that followed the strict French quality of Versailles. Sculptures and joke fountains have also been used to give amusement in Elizabethan, Italian, Moorish and Rococo gardens.

Only a handful of modern gardens exist where a display of contemporary sculpture is a primary concern, although this is gradually changing, as the effect of combining sculptural aspects within a garden space, instead of the dryness of an interior or museum, can be breathtaking.

In smaller or more modest gardens, sculptural aspects are often provided by garden ornaments, fountains, bird baths and stones.

Sculpture and ornament can be useful within an embroidered garden, offering form and a focus of attention, and a human interest and scale to the textures and colours of the garden. The sculpture can also be used to 'say' something about the view and bring meaning to an embroidery.

Climbing and hanging gardens, and gardens as hangings

Weeping, creeping and hanging gardens are becoming increasingly popular, even though their origins date back to the long disappeared 'Hanging gardens of Babylon', which were probably more terraced than hanging.

From hanging baskets on a small scale to huge climbing plants secured against a wall or hiding a shed, such plants can add extra colour and interest to a garden, and the mixture of structure and foliage or flower can provide inspiration for embroidery.

Hanging baskets make an excellent starting point for a piece based on mixed stumpwork techniques, and climbing or hanging plants contrasted against architectural detail can look effective, as in the piece *Le Parc des Moutiers – an Impression*.

Flowers and climbers around a door can make a pretty scene, or a few clematis flowers drawn against a stone wall may be a starting point for a simple three-dimensional embroidery.

At Barnsley House, near Cirencester in Gloucestershire, a laburnum tunnel hangs down, giving way to wisteria towards the outside of the arches. Bodnant in Wales boasts a similar, though even larger, arch. Richard Box's *Wisteria* painting and embroidery are reproduced in the colour photographs on pages 22 and 23; below are some notes on the conception of these pieces which give one artist's insight on how drawing can lead into embroidery design.

Richard Box paints directly from the subject in order to respond to the wisteria flowers themselves in their situation. By being there it is possible to experience

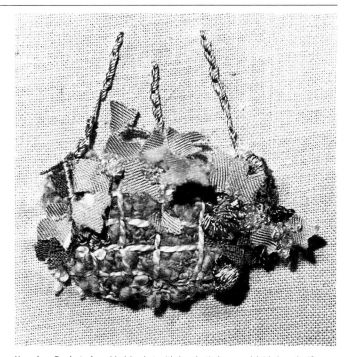

Hanging Basket. A padded basket with hand stitchery and laid threads (Sonya Head)

Hanging basket. A padded embroidery worked by machine on vanishing fabric (Sian Kibblewhite)

colour, in all its variety, changing light and tonal values, the rhythms and patterns of the twisting branches and even the bird-song! The effect of the sunlight and breeze on the artist as well as the wisteria are equally important as part of the total experience. Because drawing and painting are a process of discovery, many studies must be engaged in concurrently as this helps in trying more ways of expressing responses to a subject. Painting and drawing are done first for their own sake, and studies chosen for an embroidery afterwards. The painting chosen will go some way towards affecting the chosen responses to the image, as well as having a balanced composition and harmony.

Textiles and embroidery are chosen by Richard to further the experience of a scene because of the enjoyment and excitement of mixing and juxtaposing various threads and fabrics. Richard Box's method of embroidery includes collageing with many and varied fabrics and adding machine stitchery to create a harmony and occasional pick out line, and hand stitching to increase textural effects and pick out detail. Many colours are required: for example, in the *Wisteria* nearly thirty different tones and hues of purple are used!

Gardens in miniature

Alpine gardens and rockeries worked as miniatures of a natural environment are a fairly recent invention, but an early example of flowers set within a wall for decorative effect exists in manuscripts relating to Hampton Court, where rosemary was 'so planted and nailed to the walls as to cover them entirely'.

William Robinson (1839–1935) is credited with bringing the notion of the Alpine garden to England, an idea that was made more popular by his book *Alpine Flowers for English Gardens* (1870). In it he expounded the virtues of the Alpine garden made in a pseudo-mountain setting amongst gravel and rocks, and containing the often very tiny plants discovered in Switzerland, Scandinavia and the Pyrenees. Rockeries became the late-Victorian answer, where the neatness of small plants was swamped in beds of larger growth, with rocks and boulders positioned intermittently.

Alpine gardens, rockeries and other miniature gardens such as window boxes, hanging baskets and indoor gardens are always popular and abound today.

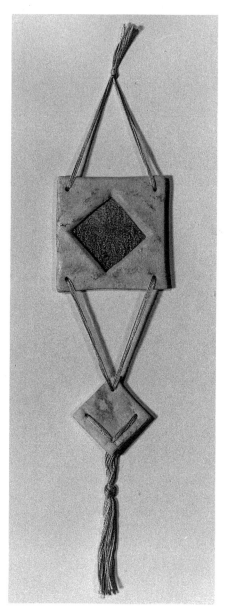

Cross-stitch Garden. Worked on porcelain coloured with underglazes and holed for the stitches. The stitches and cord are worked in silk (by the author)

Porcelain tile with machine embroidered centre on dyed silk. The bead is also porcelain. The hanging threads and tassel are of silk (by the author)

Window Box. Worked on a batik silk ground with machine stitching and vanishing fabric flowers and leaves (Sian Kibblewhite)

Wall garden. Worked on a dyed silk noile background with a variety of stitches in stranded cottons (Sheila Barrow)

Window Box. Worked on a batik silk ground with machine stitching and vanishing fabric leaves and flowers (Sian Kibblewhite)

For the embroiderer they have many advantages associated with a preconceived aspect and possibly a semi-vertical setting wherein colour, texture, shape and form mix together to create a surface interest where any considerations of depth will be minimal. It is important, however, to choose carefully the garden that is to be drawn to ensure that there is enough interest for both the drawing and the embroidery that will follow. Miniature gardens in window boxes and hanging baskets can be attractive subject matter where a foil of architectural order is used for an unruly mass of embroidered plants and flowers.

The conservatory garden

Although many gardens in the past had rooms within them, the concept of a garden within a room seems relatively new. Courtyard gardens could often give a feeling of a room and this is most effective in Mediterranean and Moorish gardens.

In Elizabethan times the need plants have for warmth, particularly for protection from winter frosts, was known, and 'stoves' were built in gardens to accommodate this need. Unfortunately the importance of light to plants was not understood, and 'stoves' and even some 'orangeries' often resembled heated cellars. Bicton Park, near Budleigh Salterton in Devon, has the oldest as well as one of the most handsome nineteenth-century conservatories. Today it contains many tender plants, but it was built tall enough for palms and other exotica.

Today many beautiful conservatories can be seen, particularly at botanical gardens, where collections of exotic plants and palms often combine with pools and fountains in order to keep the conservatory humid. Such rooms offer excellent places for drawing. Unlike gardens, the weather is predictable, and when visited out of season or during the week, privacy can often be found for drawing projects. Working with line, tone and shape, or colour and shape, drawings can be created for future work where pattern, shape or the intersection of shapes can become the key points of interest. Where pools or fountains are included a composition can become relaxing and cool.

Many homes have small areas given over to plants, or conservatories which bridge the gap between the house and garden or patio. Windows may become gardens in themselves, covered in pot plants or shrouded in hanging baskets. Here, embroideries could concentrate on the effects of light from the outside against the darkness inside, or vice versa if studied at night. Another popular approach is to look through a window to a garden view. The plants on the inside of the window, with their scale and detail, can be contrasted to the more general mass of colour seen through the window. The nature of the window itself can also add interest.

Plants within a conservatory can be of a quite different nature from those outside. Often the leaves are larger, as well as more exotic in shape. These shapes can appear more clearly defined than those in a garden, and are therefore a good starting point for design.

Furnishings within a conservatory can add interest to drawings and embroideries, adding form and an architectural dimension to a drawing which may otherwise be just a collection of patterns of shapes. The shapes of many old and modern conservatories make an elegant framework within which to set an embroidery, which again will add structure to the work. There are a number of colour photographs on conservatory themes (pages 46, 47, 62, and 70).

The vegetable garden

Vegetable gardens created for personal consumption rather than the market have been in existence for as long as people have been cultivating vegetables.

Under the feudal system, every man had his lord for whom he slaved (unless he had a craft and lived in a town with a charter). In return he was allowed to cultivate strips of land in the open fields of the manor, and given meadow and grazing rights.

Vegetable potagers were also often established close to the manor for consumption by the lord. These were often established in knot gardens so as to look attractive, but their proximity to the manor meant that they were protected from thieves. These ancient gardens can often be found as maintained or reconstructed walled kitchen gardens in many places open to the public: perhaps the most remarkable is at Villandry in France.

The feudal rights to a strip of land began to disappear in the sixteenth century with the closure of the manorial commons; but, although inadequate, cottagers were given 'allotments' which were usually attached to their cottages, and in which a few vegetables could be cultivated. It is from these that the cottage garden evolved.

By the early nineteenth century a few landowners were providing allotments voluntarily, and parishes would let some of their available land, but it was insufficient to meet the need. The General Enclosure Act of 1845 finally provided up to a quarter of an acre for individuals to cultivate – it being thought that moral good came of working on the land – but it came too late, as most of the land was already enclosed.

In spite of this, allotments were on the increase, and the two World Wars saw an astonishing rise in the number being worked. In the Second World War in

Sample for a kitchen garden, worked directly on to dyed silk wadding with free machine embroidery. The dyeing was done with a 2 cm (¾ in) flat soft brush (by the author)

Sample for a kitchen garden. Fibre-tip dyes on silk with water added and free machine embroidery worked over (by the author)

Close-up of stitched centre of **Secret Garden** embroidery. With the exception of a very few french knots on the grass, this piece was worked entirely by machine using many different tensions and a few different stitches (by the author)

England, Holland, and Germany, areas previously set aside for leisure came into use in 'Dig for Victory' and similar campaigns.

Allotments are now officially called 'leisure gardens' and some are run on the Dutch model, where within the environs of a city people may have a small patch of garden with a summer house for pleasure use. Since the war, allotments have had a chequered history, going through phases of neglect and over-subscription, but most English allotments these days still retain the essential character of a vegetable plot.

Vegetable gardens and allotments should not be ignored as inspiration for embroidery. In cottage gardens vegetables were often interspersed with herbs and flowers which had properties that warded off slugs and other pests. Vegetables, fruit and herbs may have been grown to supply a need, but there was no reason why the garden created should not be as attractive as possible, contain colour and give off pleasant smells. The result offers an interesting collection of shapes and colours, the varying greens of vegetables against the occasional flower or flowering herb. Cottage gardens were traditionally grown in slightly raised beds behind planks, bricks, stone or box hedging, and the overall effect is one of contrast – the attempts at order trying to control disorder and the fruitfulness of the growing garden which covers every available space in an effort to keep down weeds and provide for the cottager's needs.

The apparently haphazard nature of planting in the traditional cottage garden is in marked contrast to the planting that is now associated with vegetable plots and allotments, although these nevertheless have their own charm. Allotments can be viewed as rows and rows of different patches, interspersed with sheds, tools, pathways, trellising, canes, scarecrows or the odd fence or hedge. This can make an interesting subject for a textile of irregularly repeated motifs – perhaps using patchwork or appliqué. Vegetable gardens seen individually offer a variety of shape and form. They may offer perspective challenges as rows of vegetables or standing canes recede from the viewer. The viewpoint may be low, looking along the ground, along the rows of vegetables or through archways of canes, giving a heightened sense of perspective, or try looking down on allotments from a vantage point to discover a quality of pattern and order.

The patterns of the vegetable garden can be pleasing and orderly, and if combined with three-dimensional embroidery or stumpwork, as on examples of Peruvian contemporary panels, it can be charming and amusing. The patterns and shapes derived from allotments can be adapted and drawn and re-drawn to create a more abstracted appearance. This can evoke an impression of allotments with their fruitfulness and vegetation, without being specific and repetitive. Placed within a context, it may be possible to evoke the notion of an edible retreat, perhaps within the confines of a city.

Now we return to the quotation at the beginning of the chapter. The carriage has journeyed this far, and it is time to walk on foot. May I wish you 'Bon Voyage'; may your journey be pleasurable and exciting. Remember, most of all, that the journey is as important as the goal, and is often more enlightening.

FURTHER READING

Where to find gardens

Gardens of England and Wales. A complete list of private gardens open in aid of The National Gardens Scheme, Benham & Co

Pearson, Mitchel and Gibbs, *The Ordnance Survey guide to gardens in Britain*, Country Life Books

Photography

Partridge, Joe, *One-touch photography: a guide to compact auto-focus cameras*, Pan

Hedgecoe, John, *The photographer's handbook*, Ebury Press

Freeman, Michael, *Collins photography workshop: cameras and lenses*, Collins

Freeman, Michael, *Collins photography workshop: the image*, Collins

Drawing and painting

Brown, David, *Draw perspective*, A & C Black

Woods, Michael, *Perspective in art*, Batsford

Vincer, Carol, *Draw your garden*, A & C Black

Itten, Johannes, *The elements of colour*, Van Nostrand Reinhold

Simpson, Ian, *Painter's progress*, Phoebe Phillips Editions

Embroidery

Butler, Ann, *The Batsford encyclopaedia of embroidery stitches*, Batsford

Beaney, Jan, *Embroidery: new approaches*, Pelham Books

Howard, Constance, *The Constance Howard book of stitches*, Batsford

Campbell-Harding, Valerie, *Flowers and plants in embroidery*, Batsford

McNeill, Moyra, *Machine embroidery: lace and see-through techniques*, Batsford

Rhodes, Mary, *Dictionary of canvas work stitches*, Batsford

Messent, Jan, *The embroiderer's workbook*, Batsford

Beck, Thomasina, *The embroiderer's garden*, David and Charles

LIST OF SUPPLIERS

Many of the following will supply mail order; most will send a price list on receipt of an SAE.

Creative Beadcraft Ltd
Unit 26
Chiltern Trading Estate
Holmer Green
High Wycombe
Bucks
(Beads)

Campden Needlecraft Centre
High Street
Chipping Campden
Gloucestershire
(An extensive range of embroidery fabrics and threads – complete ranges stocked, including coloured scrims)

Borovicks
16 Berwick Street
London W1
(Wide range of fabrics, including transparent ones)

Silken Strands
33 Linksway
Gatley
Cheadle
Cheshire
SK8 4LA
(Machine embroidery
threads)

The Handworker's Market
The Shire Hall
Shirehall Plain
Holt
Norfolk
NR25 6BG
(Embroidery supplies)

Whaleys (Bradford) Ltd
Harris Court
Great Horton
Bradford
West Yorks
(Water-soluble and
vanishing muslin (minimum
order))

Russells
30 Castle Street
Carlisle
(Embroidery threads)

In Stitches
48 Kings Road
Brentwood
Essex
(Embroidery supplies)

Voirrey Embroidery
Brimstage Hall
Brimstage
Wirral
L62 6JA
(Embroidery supplies,
exhibitions and courses)

Sue Harris
The Mill
Tregoyd Mill
Three Cocks
Brecon
Powys
LD3 0SW
(Silk wadding)

Sarah Beecham
The Almonry
Chipping Campden
Gloucestershire
(Canvas work design)

More suppliers can be found
in *Embroidery*, a quarterly
magazine published by the
Embroiderers' Guild
Circulation Dept
PO Box 42B
East Molesey, Surrey KT8

Embroiderers' Guild addresses

UK
The Embroiderers' Guild
Apartment 41A
Hampton Court
East Molesey
Surrey
KT6 9AU

USA
The Embroiderers' Guild of America
200 Fourth Avenue
Louiseville
Kentucky
40202

Australia
The Embroiderers' Guild of Australia
175 Elizabeth Street
Sydney
New South Wales 2000

New Zealand
Association of New Zealand Embroiderers' Guild
171 The Ridgeway
Mornington
Wellington 2

Canada
Canadian Embroiderers' Guild
PO Box 541
Station B
London
Ontario
N6A 4W1

INDEX

NB Entries in italics refer to illustrations.